Lifestyle Designs
13720 460th CT. SE
NORTH BEND, WA 98045-8866

Lifestyle Designs
13720 460th CT. SE
NORTH BEND, WA 98045-8866

DESIGNS
FOR
WINDOW
TREATMENTS

*Over 100 Styles for Curtains
and other Soft Furnishings*

Also by Lady Caroline Wrey

THE COMPLETE BOOK OF CURTAINS AND DRAPES

THE COMPLETE BOOK OF BEDROOM ELEGANCE

DESIGNS
FOR
WINDOW
TREATMENTS

*Over 100 Styles for Curtains and
other Soft Furnishings*

Lady Caroline Wrey

THE OVERLOOK PRESS
WOODSTOCK · NEW YORK

First published in the United States in 1995 by
The Overlook Press
Lewis Hollow Road
Woodstock, New York 12498

Text copyright © Caroline Wrey
Illustrations copyright © Vana Haggerty 1995

Library of Congress Cataloging-in-Publication Data
Wrey, Caroline, 1957 –
    Designs for window treatments: 100 styles for curtains, draperies. and other sewn furnishing /
Lady Caroline Wrey.
        p. cm.
    Includes index.
    1. Drapery. 2. Drapery in interior decoration. 3. House furnishings. 4. Sewing. I. Title.
    TT390.W693 1995
    646.2'1-dc20
                                                                                        94-37357
                                                                                        CIP

ISBN: 0-87951-585-6
Printed in Portugal by Printer Portuguesa Lda
135798642

CONTENTS

Acknowledgements

This book is entirely due to my husband, George, who inspired me to produce it. Having been given the idea, I began to realise that there was a complete gap in the market which this type of book could fill. I am so grateful for all his encouragement and that of Ebury Press. My thanks also to Margot Richardson's brilliant editing skills and Vana Haggerty's superbly skilled and detailed drawings.

The imperial and metric measurement used in this book are not exact conversions of each other, and therefore the two systems of measurement should not be used interchangeably.

Introduction

I am passionately interested in designing and making window treatments and other soft furnishings, and continually think about new designs, and how to create interesting new looks for the home.

My previous two books – *The Complete Book of Curtains and Drapes* and *The Complete Book of Bedroom Elegance* – are entirely practical. They contain comprehensive instructions on how to plan, cut out and sew curtains, pelmets, Austrian and Roman blinds, tiebacks, table covers and bed valances, etc. By using those books, anyone with some sewing ability can easily make a range of fabulous home furnishings.

However, despite having covered these subjects in detail, I felt there was a real need for a different sort of book, to help people – and not just those who can sew – to plan and design their furnishings more easily.

I feel that the hardest part of an interior design project is the measuring up and actual design work, but this book guides you totally through those initial stages, giving an exact formula, instructions and list of 'ingredients' in straightforward text.

There are tips on the best use of particular designs, the desirable proportions in any room setting, and the quantity of material needed. You can then decide whether a particular design is suitable for the purpose you

had in mind and, because the amount of material is specified, even calculate the cost of the design.

Each project or item is illustrated with a simple but totally accurate line drawing, so that you can see all the elements of the design, but picture it in your own room and in your preferred fabric.

This book gives you, in plain black and white, the solution for every soft-furnishing situation. Once you have used it to plan your projects, everything will be so easy. I hope this book will become invaluable for both amateurs and professionals alike, and that using it to create a beautiful home will be as rewarding for you as it has been for me.

LADY CAROLINE WREY

Curtains

1
PLAIN WINDOW WITH PELMET BOARD

This is the basic pelmet/curtain-hanging board needed for almost every type of window treatment. You do not need to paint the board, but it looks very professional if you do.

1 **Board depth:** 17cm/6¾in (always) unless window is particularly small.

2 **Board thickness:** 2cm/¾in.

3 **Board length:** Should overlap window (architrave to architrave) by about 10 per cent, on either side.

4 **Curtain rail:** Top-quality metal type with cords. It should be the same length as the pelmet board, 3 above.

5 **Pulley system:** Absolutely essential, and ideally finished with brass acorns and not the plastic tensioner supplied with the rails (which is designed to be screwed into your skirting board behind the curtains). However, if your window is particularly wide and low then you have to use the tensioner.

6 **Brass screw eye:** Two, either end of board, 3–4cm/1¼–1½in long, if possible.
It is vital that your curtain comes off the end of the rail and turns a right angle into the wall and then hugs it. There should be no dreadful gap between the wall and the curtain.

7 **Velcro:** 2cm/¾in wide. The only way to hang all pelmets (bar parts of swags and tails). Attach using a staple gun only: do not use the self-adhesive type as it is not strong enough.

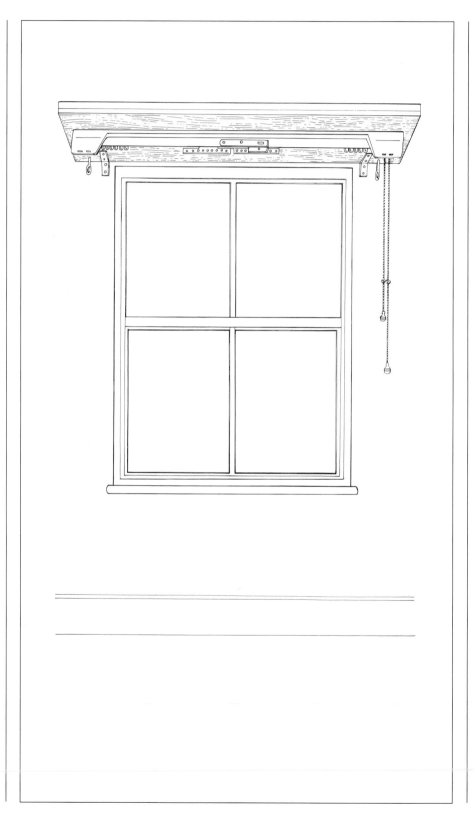

2
BASIC PENCIL-PLEATED CURTAINS

This is the basic type of curtain heading which goes under all pelmets, but it is not designed to be exposed in any way. However, this 8cm/3¼in pencil-pleated heading looks excellent on a fixed pelmet or static curtain.

1 **Width of each finished, gathered curtain:** Half width of window, plus central overlap distance, and return to wall on either side, (which is usually 17cm/6¾in in total).

2 **Width of each finished, flat curtain:** Half width of window, plus central overlap distance, × approx. 2.5 for gathering.

3 **Unsewn width of each curtain:** As 2 above (half width of window, plus central overlap distance, × 2.5 for gathering) plus 10cm/4in for turn-backs (5cm/2in) at each side).

4 **Length of pencil-pleat gathering tape:** As 2 above (half width of window, plus central overlap distance, × 2.5 for gathering) plus 2cm/¾in either end for the turning in of tape.

5 **Finished drop for each curtain:** Height from bottom of pelmet board to floor, less 2cm/¾in allowance for the rail fixed below the board.

6 **Unsewn drop for each curtain:** Height as 5 above (from curtain rod to floor) plus 20cm/8in for both turn-down at top (8cm/3¼in) and hem at bottom (12cm/4¾in). If the material has a pattern, remember to allow extra for pattern repeats: add on one pattern repeat per drop cut.

7 **Lining quantity:** As unsewn width 3 and unsewn drop 6 above less 10cm/4in.

8 **Interlining quantity:** As lining, 7 above.

3
SINGLE FRENCH-PLEAT CURTAINS

With covered fascia board

The perfect window treatment in the following situations:
• *Where a simple, understated look is needed and a pelmet would look wrong.*
• *Where there is a complete lack of any ceiling clearance, and there is no housing space for curtains either side of the window (due to adjacent walls, or cupboard doors). This would make it impossible to use a curtain pole, and/or finials at the ends.*
• *Where you cannot afford to lose any light whatsoever; therefore a plain curtain rail, disguised by a fascia, is the perfect solution.*

1 **Width of finished, pleated curtain:** Half the width of the covered fascia board plus: central overlap distance, return into the wall, and 2cm/¾in per pleat. (This extra is to allow for the essential 'spring back' between each pleat.)

2 **Width of each finished, flat curtain (before pleating):** Half the width of the covered fascia board × 2.5 for pleating, plus central overlap distance and return to the wall.

3 **Unsewn width of each curtain:** As 2 above (half the width of the covered fascia board × 2.5 for pleating, plus centre overlap distance) plus 10cm/4in for turn-backs (5cm/2in at each side).

4 **Length of fusible buckram:** As 2 above: half the width the covered fascia board × 2.5 for pleating, plus centre overlap distance. Insert the fusible buckram between the lining and interlining and fuse with a hot iron.

5 **Finished drop for each curtain:** Height from top of the covered fascia board to the floor.

6 **Unsewn drop for each curtain:** Height from the top of the covered fascia board to the floor, plus a total of 30cm/12in (12cm/4¾in for the hem and 18cm/7in for the top). If the material has a pattern, remember to allow extra for pattern repeats: add on one pattern repeat per drop cut.

7 **Lining quantity:** Height from top of covered fascia board to floor, plus 12cm/4¾in for the hem.

8 **Interlining quantity:** As 7 above, but plus 9cm/3½in for the hem.

4
GOBLET-PLEATED CURTAINS ON A POLE

With contrast buttons

This curtain suits any type of window except, perhaps, tiny cottage windows. The beauty of this treatment is that there is no light loss at all because there is no pelmet. It is therefore particularly suitable for a north- or east-facing window where a pelmet would block valuable light. For an average-sized window the goblet pleats should be formed 12cm/5in wide and about 12cm/5in apart. You will need one contrast-bound button per pleat.

1 **Width of each finished, pleated curtain:** Half width of pole, plus centre overlap distance if needed, and return to wall on either side. Also add 2cm/¾in allowance per pleat, to allow for the essential 'spring back' between each pleat.

2 **Width of each finished, flat curtain (before pleating):** Half the width of the pole × 2.5 for pleating.

3 **Unsewn width of each curtain:** As 2 above (half width of pole × 2.5) plus 10cm/4in for turn-backs (5cm/2in at each side).

4 **Length of fusible buckram:** As 2 above: half width of pole × 2.5 for pleating. Insert the buckram between the lining and interlining.

5 **Finished drop for each curtain:** Height from screw eye in wooden ring to floor. The easiest way to measure this is to tie a piece of string on to the screw eye and pull it taut, without stretching it, to the floor. Measure the length of the string.

6 **Unsewn drop for each curtain:** Height from the screw eye to floor plus a total of 30cm/12in: 12cm/5in for the hem and 18cm/7in for the turn-down at the top. Remember to allow extra for pattern repeats, if the material has a pattern.

7 **Lining quantity:** Height from screw eye to floor, plus 12cm/5in for the hem.

8 **Interlining quantity:** Height from screw eye to floor.

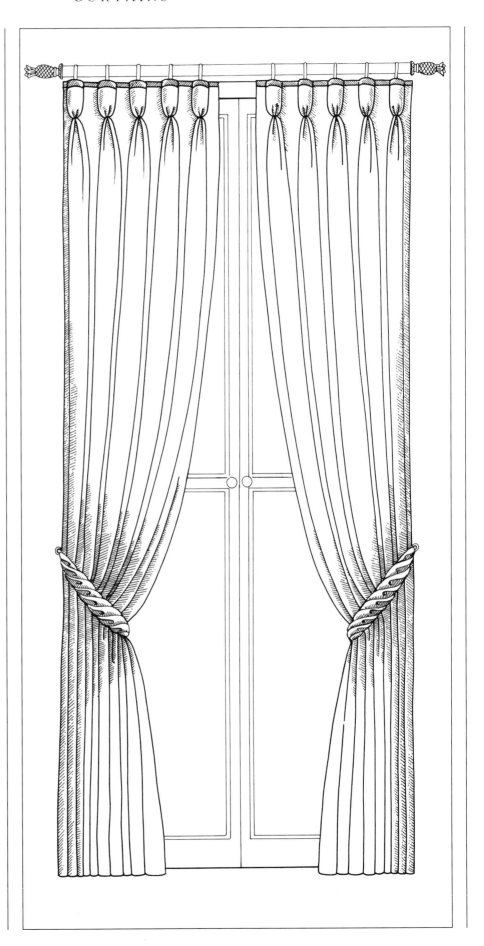

5
PUFF-BALL HEADING OFF A POLE

With contrast-bound top and leading edges

A very beautiful heading with a powerful character. It looks best if the heading is kept static, that is, the curtains are opened using some sort of tie-back but not by moving the rings/ runners.

It is essential that a contrast colour is used in the top section and on the leading edges since this detail literally 'makes' the success of the window treatment.

Use heavy dacron as wadding material in the top 12cm/4¾in above the narrow Rufflette heading, thus allowing the top to flop over into an effective 'puff ball'.

1 **Width of finished, pleated curtain:** Half the width of the pole plus the return into the wall.

2 **Width of each finished, flat curtain (before pleating):** Half the width of the pole × 2.5 to allow for gathering.

3 **Unsewn width of each curtain:** As 2 above (half the width of the pole × 2.5 for gathering) plus 10cm/4in for turn-backs at sides (5cm/2in at each side).

4 **Length of (narrow, 3cm/1¼in) gathering tape:** Length as 2 above (half the width of the pole × 2.5). Machine stitch the tape 13cm/5in below the top of the curtain, exactly below where the contrast (and the heavy dacron) start.

5 **Finished drop for each curtain:** Height from screw eye in the wooden ring to the floor, plus 24cm/9½in of contrast for the puff ball at the top: 12cm/4¾in to show on right side, and 12cm/4¾in to go down the back.

6 **Unsewn drop for each curtain:** As 5 above, plus 39cm/15¼in: 12cm/4¾in for the hem at the bottom (in the main material), and 24cm/9½in further of contrast so that when it 'puffballs' over, you see the contrast on both sides. (This includes a small seam allowance of 1.5cm/ ⅝in.)

7 **Lining quantity:** Height from screw eye to floor, plus 3cm/1¼in: there is a 6cm/2¼in hem, but the lining sits 3cm/

1¼in above the finished hem of the curtain.

8 **Interlining quantity:** As 7 above, but plus 9cm/3½in for the hem.

9 **Contrast binding for leading edge:** Cut a 13cm/5in strip (4cm/1½in of this will be folded back over itself, ie, using up 8cm/3in, and then 5cm/2in will be the leading edge turning) × the total length of the curtain (inclusive of the hem and 12cm/4¾in contrast at the top). Machine stitch this 4cm/1½in away from the raw edge of the curtain material, thus achieving a 4cm/1½in border. You can also make this into a wadded edge by adding 8cm/ 3in of heavy dacron, folded in half.

6
SLOTTED, POLE-HEADED CURTAIN

With Maltese cross

These are essentially fixed-head or static curtains designed not to be pulled, but to be held back at either side by tie-backs or brass hold-backs, thus allowing light through. Do not consider this window treatment if you need light in your room (and if it faces north or east). However, it is particularly fitting in, for example, halls or landings, or even more especially if the window faces south or west and is not too dark.

It is also sometimes a good idea not to use interlining as you then get a wonderful effect from the light bringing out the best quality of the design of the material. If, however, you do use interlining, it must stop at the lowest machine line of the channel for the curtain pole, otherwise it would be too bulky and also would ruin the look of the sharp stand-up.

1 Width of each finished, gathered curtain (once slotted onto curtain pole): Half width of window.

2 Width of each finished, flat curtain: Half width of window × 3 (for the desired fullness and ruched effect on the pole).

3 Unsewn width of each curtain: As 2 above (half width of window × 3) plus 10cm/4in for turn-backs (5cm/2in at each side).

4 Length of gathering tape/fusible buckram: Not applicable.

5 Finished drop for each curtain: Height from bottom of pole to the floor, plus the channel for the pole (approx. double the pole's diameter), plus the desired stand-up: this depends slightly on the size of the pole, but double the stitched channel, or 5–8cm/2–3¼in, are good guides.

6 Unsewn drop for each curtain: Height of 5 above (from bottom of pole to floor, plus pole channel and stand-up), plus turn-down at top (same as stand-up and pole channel), plus 1cm/⅜in turn-under. This window treatment is one of the few instances when if you cut the curtain slightly too long it looks good.

7 Lining quantity: As unsewn width, 3 (half width of window × 3, plus 10cm/4in); but the height from the top of the pole to the bottom of the finished curtain less 3cm/1¼in, plus a 6cm/2¼in allowance for the hem.

8 Interlining quantity: As unsewn width 3, and length 7.

9 Maltese cross: See no 81.

7
POLE-HEADED CURTAINS ON BRASS ROD

With contrast channel and inset piped frill

This type of heading looks especially good on a small window, as the use of a small rod (approx 1cm/⅜in diameter) for the heading makes less impact than a large, solid wooden pole. This treatment also looks good when curtains have to be short due to units or furniture that come up to the window sill.

As well, all the characteristics of no 5 apply to this type of treatment.

1 **Width of each finished, gathered curtain** (once slotted onto curtain pole): Half width of window.

2 **Width of each finished, flat curtain:** Half width of window × 3 (for the desired fullness and ruched effect on the pole).

3 **Unsewn width of each curtain:** As 2 above (half width of window × 3) plus 10cm/4in for turn-backs (5cm/2in at each side).

4 **Length of gathering tape/fusible buckram:** Not applicable.

5 **Finished drop for each curtain:** Height from bottom of pole to the floor, plus the channel for the pole (approx. double the pole's diameter), plus the desired stand-up: this depends slightly on the size of the pole, but double the stitched channel or 5–8cm/2–3¼in are good guides.

6 **Unsewn drop for each curtain:** Height of 5 above (from bottom of pole to floor, plus pole channel and stand-up), plus turn-down at top (same as stand-up and pole channel), plus 1cm/⅜in turn-under.

7 **Lining quantity:** As unsewn width, 3 (half width of window × 3, plus 10cm/4in); but the height from the top of the pole to the bottom of the finished curtain less 3cm/1¼in, plus a 6cm/2¼in allowance for the hem.

8 **Interlining quantity:** As unsewn width 3, and length 7.

9 **Contrast channel:** Machine stitch on a contrast-coloured strip, the same width as the channel. The strip should be made of double fabric, with a seam down its centre at the back.

10 **Bow tie-back:** See no 77.

8

ITALIAN-STRUNG CURTAINS ON A GENTLY CURVING BOARD

Another static-head design that is effective and eye-catching. Curtains hung in this way are best used as 'dress' curtains, and not continually opened and closed.

The window should be slim: not less than 2.1m/7ft high, and not wider than about 1.3m/4ft 3in (architrave to architrave). The finished look is visually interesting, not only because of the curved top, but also because of the 'invisible' method of being held back, that is, the Italian stringing. The curve of the board is only about 15cm/6in at its highest point, so the curtains do not need to be cut on a template: they are cut completely straight.

1 **Width of each finished, gathered curtain:** Exactly half the total width of the curved top of the board.

2 **Width of each finished, flat curtain:** As 1 (half the width of the board) × 2.5 or 3, depending on the fullness required.

3 **Unsewn width of each curtain:** As 2 (half the width of the board × 2.5/3) plus 10cm/4in for turn-backs (5cm/2in at each side).

4 **Length of pencil-pleat gathering tape:** As 2 above (half the width of the board × 2.5/3) plus 2cm/¾in either end for turning in of tape.

5 **Finished drop for each curtain:** The top of each curtain is cut completely straight. It is purely the adaptability of pencil-pleat tape that enables the heading to curve with ease round the curved board. Therefore the drop at each outer edge of the curtain comes to the floor but the bottom edges at the centre will not be on the floor but 15cm/6in above.

6 **Unsewn drop for each curtain:** As 5 above, plus 20cm/8in: 8cm/3¼in for turnings for the pencil-pleated heading, and 12cm/4¾in for the hem at the bottom.

7 **Lining quantity:** As 2 and 5 above less 10cm/4in.

8 **Interlining quantity:** As 7 above.

9 **Stringing:** Before pulling up the pencil pleats sew a plastic ring on the back of the flat curtain, between ¼ and ⅓ of the way down from the top and close to the leading edge. Stitch rings 10cm/4in apart in a diagonal line sloping up at approx. 45 degrees from the first ring.

9
CURTAINS ON BRASS SWING ARMS

With inset frill

A very suitable treatment for a window in a recess or a dormer window. In these situations ordinary curtains would block out too much light as there is no housing space available to pull the curtains away from the window. An Austrian blind would also block out far too much light, as would a Roman blind, so this is the perfect solution. The pair of brass swing arms and their wall fittings are elegant in appearance. As both sides of the curtain are seen in the room, main fabric is used on both sides, rather than lining on the exterior side.

1 **Width of each finished, gathered curtain** (when ruched onto the arm): Exact width of one of the swing arms.

2 **Width of each finished, flat curtain:** Width of one swing arm × 2. (More than double makes them too full.)

3 **Unsewn width of each curtain:** As 2 above (width of one swing arm × 2) plus 3cm/1¼in (1.5cm/⅝in seam allowance at each side).

4 **Length of gathering tape/fusible buckram:** Not applicable.

5 **Finished drop for each curtain:** Measure from bottom of swing arm to window sill then add on 2.5cm/1in for rod channel and 5cm/2in for stand-up above rod.

6 **Unsewn drop for each curtain:** As 5 above plus 5cm/2in for the bottom hem, and 1.5cm/⅝in seam allowance at the top

to attach the second drop of fabric for the other side of the curtain.

7 **Lining quantity:** As 6 above, but use main fabric, not lining.

8 **Interlining quantity:** The exact drop from rod to sill plus 2cm/¾in seam allowance. (Once the interlining is machine stitched in place, trim it right back to the lowest line of stitching that forms the channel for the swing arm.)

9 **Length of gathered, finished frill:** As 5 above (finished drop of curtain). (See no 103.)

Variation: Pipe the frill with a contrast colour, on both sides of the curtain, so that piping can be seen when the swing arms are both flat against the window and swung out at 90 degrees to the window. (See no 106.)

10
LOFT WINDOW CURTAINS ON TWO BRASS RODS

One of the very few solutions for a Velux (loft) window in a sloping roof, carried out by fixing brass drop rods above and below the window. Making the curtains with a stand-up above and below adds a pretty finishing touch.

The curtains are hung on the rods with brass split rings which are attached to the curtain with narrow 3cm/1¼in tape stitched 5cm/2in below the top and above the bottom of the curtain.

1 **Width of each finished, gathered curtain:** Half the width of one rod .

2 **Width of each finished, flat curtain:** As 1 above (half the width of the rod) × 2: ie the same width as the length of the rod.

3 **Unsewn width of each curtain:** As 2 above (the length of the rod) plus 10cm/4in for turn-backs (5cm/2in at each side).

4 **Length of gathering tape:** As 2 above (total length of the rod) plus 2cm/¾in either end for turning in of tape.

5 **Finished drop for each curtain:** Exact measurement from top rod to bottom rod, plus 10cm/4in (5cm/2in stand-up at top and bottom).

6 **Unsewn drop for each curtain:** Top rod to bottom rod plus 26cm/10¼in: 12cm/4¾in allowance at both top and bottom (to achieve a 5cm/2in stand-up with main material on both sides) plus a 2cm/¾in turning.

7 **Lining quantity:** Exact measurement from top rod to bottom rod.

8 **Interlining quantity:** As 7 above.

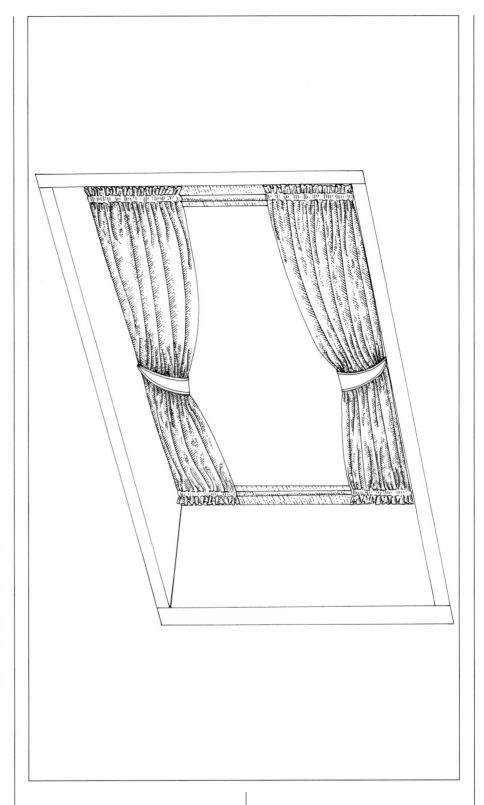

17

11

PENCIL-PLEAT PELMET

With top contrast binding and inset fringe

This is a particularly versatile type of pelmet, and very suitable in many situations – upstairs or down. The pencil pleats are pretty and reticent for a bedroom, yet they can look important in a reception room depending, for example, on which details are added to the pelmet.

For the best effect, the pelmet must always be interlined.

CURTAINS

See no 2

PELMET

1 **Width of finished, pleated pelmet:** Width of pelmet board, plus returns at either end.

2 **Width of finished, unpleated pelmet:** As 1 above (width of pelmet board plus returns) × 2.5.

3 **Unsewn width of pelmet:** As 2 above (width of pelmet board plus returns × 2.5) plus 8cm/3in for (4cm/1½in) turnings at either side.

4 **Length of 8cm/3¼in-wide pencil-pleat tape:** As 2 above (width of pelmet board plus returns × 2.5) plus 4cm/1½in (2cm/¾in either end) for turnings.

5 **Finished drop of pelmet:** Approx. ⅙ total drop of curtains.

6 **Unsewn drop of pelmet:** As 5 above (⅙ total drop of curtains) plus 6cm/2⅜in: 5cm/2in for turning at top plus 1cm/⅜in for seam allowance at bottom. Cut an additional strip the same length, but 7cm/2¾in wide for the hem of the pelmet once the fringe has been inset.

7 **Lining quantity:** Width as 3 above; drop as 5 above less 4.5cm/1¾ due to hem turn-up in main material, at back.

8 **Interlining quantity:** Width as 2 above; drop as 5 above.

9 **Size of contrast:** Length as 2 above plus 2cm/¾in for turnings × 7cm/2¾in wide. Gives 1cm/⅜in showing at the top.

10 **Length of fringing:** As 2 above plus 2cm/¾in for turnings.

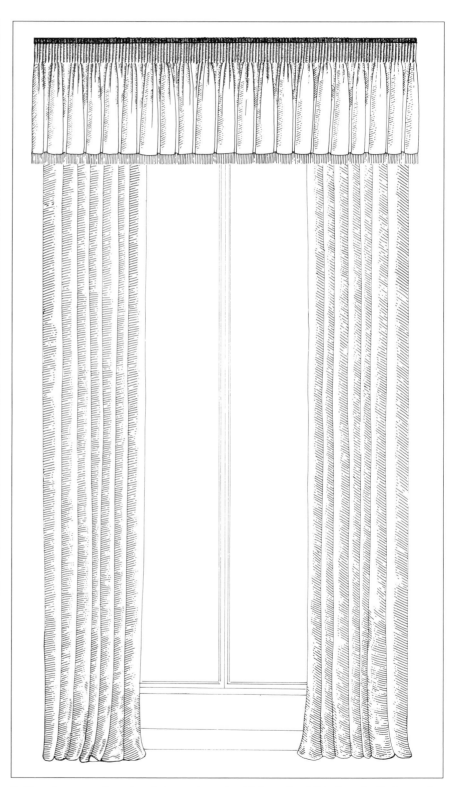

12
DEEP PENCIL-PLEAT PELMET

With a contrast-bound set-on frill

The description of no 11 also applies to this pelmet, but as this version is deeper, it makes a stronger statement than a shallower pelmet, and is more suitable for a longer drop, such as 45cm/18in.

CURTAINS

See no 2

PELMET

1 **Width of finished, pleated pelmet:** Width of pelmet board, plus returns at either end.

2 **Width of finished, unpleated pelmet:** As 1 above (width of pelmet board plus returns) × 2.5.

3 **Unsewn width of pelmet:** As 2 above (width of pelmet board plus returns × 2.5) plus 8cm/3in for (4cm/1½in) turnings at either side.

4 **Length of 15cm/6in-deep pencil-pleat tape:** As 2 above (width of pelmet board plus returns × 2.5 plus 4cm/1½in (2cm/¾in either end for turnings).

5 **Finished drop of pelmet:** Approx. ⅙ total drop of curtains.

6 **Unsewn drop of pelmet:** As 5 above (⅙ total drop of curtains), plus 11cm/4¼in: 5cm/2in for turning at top plus 6cm/2¼in for hem at bottom.

7 **Lining quantity:** Width as 3 above; drop as 5 above less 4.5cm/1¾in due to hem turn-up in main material, at back.

8 **Interlining quantity:** Width as 2 above; drop as 5 above.

9 **Frill:** See no 105.

13
FRENCH-PLEATED PELMET

With buttons, and permanent-pleated inset frill

This type of pleat makes a stronger statement than pencil pleats. They give a slightly more masculine look, although this does not mean to say that they are not suitable in a feminine situation. The button detail gives interest to the tailored pleat, and the permanent-pleated edge gives an elegant finish.

CURTAINS

See no 2

PELMET

1 **Width of finished, pleated pelmet:** Width of pelmet board, plus returns at either end.

2 **Width of finished, unpleated pelmet:** Width of pelmet board × 2.5, then add on returns at either end. (The returns are not pleated.)

3 **Unsewn width of pelmet:** As 2 above (width of board × 2.5 plus returns) plus 8cm/3in for (4cm/1½in) turnings at either side.

4 **Length of buckram:** As 2 above.

5 **Finished drop of pelmet:** Approx. ⅙ total drop of curtains.

6 **Unsewn drop of pelmet:** As 5 above (⅙ total drop of curtains), plus 16cm/6¼in: 15cm/6in for turning at top over back of buckram (but depends on depth of buckram) plus 1cm/¼in for seam allowance at bottom. Cut an additional strip the same length, but 7cm/2¾in wide for the hem of the pelmet, once the pleated trim has been inset.

7 **Lining quantity:** Width as 3 above; drop as 5 above less 4.5cm/1¾in due to hem turn-up in main material, at back.

8 **Interlining quantity:** Width as 2 above; drop as 5 above.

9 **Frill:** See no 104.

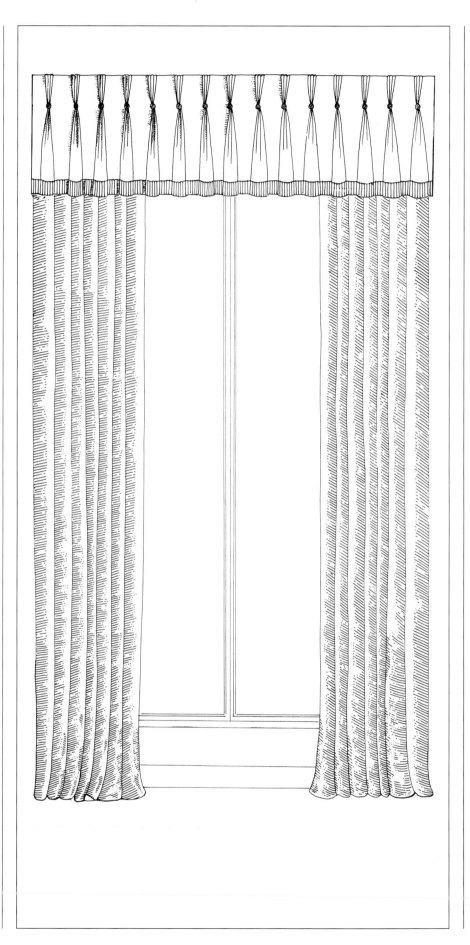

14
GOBLET-PLEATED PELMET

With swagging rope

Goblet pleats have a bolder effect than French pleats, and the swagging rope adds a greater dimension to the pelmet as a whole. This design would be highly suitable for a drawing room, dining room or elegant bedroom.

CURTAINS
See no 2

PELMET

1 Width of finished, pleated pelmet: Width of pelmet board, plus returns at either end.

2 Width of finished, unpleated pelmet: Width of pelmet board × 2.5, then add on returns at either end. (The returns are not pleated.)

3 Unsewn width of pelmet: As 2 above (width of board × 2.5 plus returns) plus 8cm/3in for (4cm/1½in) turnings at either side.

4 Length of buckram: As 2 above (width of pelmet board × 2.5 plus returns).

5 Finished drop of pelmet: Approx. ⅙ total drop of curtains.

6 Unsewn drop of pelmet: As 5 above, plus 21cm/8¼in: 15cm/6in for turning at top over back of buckram (but depends on depth of buckram) plus 6cm/2¼in for hem at bottom.

7 Lining quantity: Width as 3 above; drop as 5 above less 4.5cm/1¾in due to hem turn-up in main material, at back.

8 Interlining quantity: Width as 2 above; drop as 5 above.

9 Length of swagging rope: Allow 12cm/4¾in per knot, and then enough to loop between each pleat: this depends on the drop of the pelmet and the distance between each pleat.

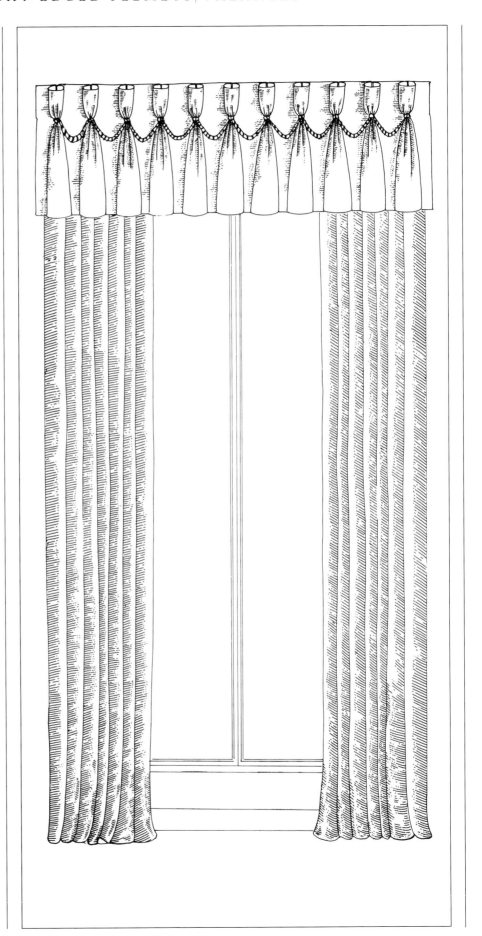

15
DIAMOND-SMOCKED PELMET

With top contrast binding

This is a beautiful, unusual and impressive heading for a pelmet. It is highly suitable for bedrooms, bathrooms, girls' bedrooms and for the tops of Austrian blinds. As well, in strong colours it is also suitable for reception rooms as it has huge presence and style.

CURTAINS

See no 2

PELMET

1 **Width of finished, pleated pelmet:** Width of pelmet board, plus returns at either end.

2 **Width of finished, unpleated pelmet:** As 1 above (width of pelmet board plus returns) × 2.

3 **Unsewn width of pelmet:** As 2 above (width of pelmet board plus returns × 2) plus 8cm/3in for (4cm/1½in) turnings at either side.

4 **Length of smocking tape:** As 2 above (width of pelmet board plus returns × 2) plus 4cm/1½in (2cm/¾in turnings at each end). Use the best-quality commercial smocking tape, 8.5cm/3¼in deep.

5 **Finished drop of pelmet:** Approx. ⅙ total drop of curtains.

6 **Unsewn drop of pelmet:** As 5 above (⅙ total drop of curtains) plus 6cm/2¼in for hem at bottom.

7 **Lining quantity:** Width as 3 above; drop as 5 above less 4.5cm/1¾in turn-up in main material, at back.

8 **Interlining quantity:** Width as 2 above; drop as 5 above.

9 **Size of contrast:** Length as 2 above (width of pelmet board plus returns × 2) plus 2cm/¾in turnings at each end); width 7cm/2¾in, which gives 1cm/⅜in showing at the top.

10 **Length of embroidery skein for smocking:** Buy 6-stranded embroidery skein to smock up the pelmet after having pulled up the smocking tape. Use all 6 strands. You will need ½ skein per material width used in the pelmet.

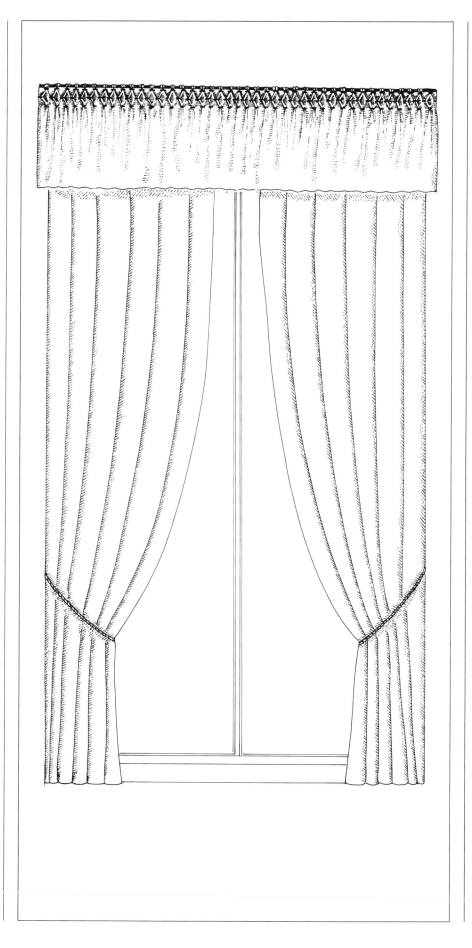

16
OUTLINED, SMOCKED PELMET

With embroidery skein and top contrast binding

This pelmet is suitable for all the areas mentioned under no 15 and is exactly the same, except for the outlining. The additional outlining gives strong geometric lines to the pelmet and, obviously, accentuates the smocking.

1 **Width of finished, pleated pelmet:** Width of pelmet board, plus returns at either end.

2 **Width of finished, unpleated pelmet:** As 1 above (width of pelmet board plus returns) × 2.

3 **Unsewn width of pelmet:** As 2 above (width of pelmet board plus returns × 2) plus 8cm/3in for (4cm/1½in) turnings at either side.

4 **Length of smocking tape:** As 2 above (width of pelmet board plus returns × 2) plus 4cm/1½in (2cm/¾in turnings at each end). Use the best-quality commercial smocking tape, 8.5cm/3¼in deep.

5 **Finished drop of pelmet:** Approx. ⅙ total drop of curtains.

6 **Unsewn drop of pelmet:** As 5 above (⅙ total drop of curtains) plus 6cm/2¼in for hem at bottom.

7 **Lining quantity:** Width as 3 above; drop as 5 above less 4.5cm/1¾in turn-up in main material, at back.

8 **Interlining quantity:** Width as 2 above; drop as 5 above.

9 **Size of contrast:** Length as 2 above (width of pelmet board plus returns × 2) plus 2cm/¾in turnings at each end); width 7cm/2¾in, which gives 1cm/⅜in showing at the top.

10 **Length of embroidery skein for smocking:** Buy 6-stranded embroidery skein to smock up the pelmet after having pulled up the smocking tape. Use all 6 strands. You will need 1¼ skein per material width.

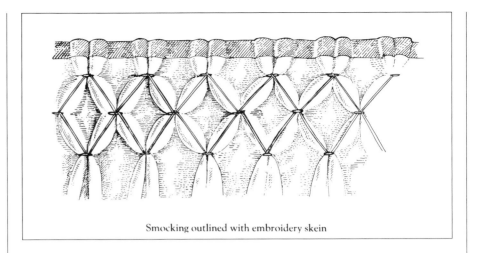

Smocking outlined with embroidery skein

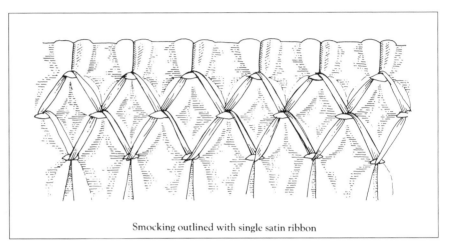

Smocking outlined with single satin ribbon

17
OUTLINED, SMOCKED PELMET

With single satin ribbon (no contrast binding)

Again, suitable for all purposes mentioned under no 15. The ribbon outline makes a strong statement.

See above for full directions.

Unsewn drop of pelmet: Approx. ⅙ total drop of curtains, plus 11cm/4¼in: 5cm/2in for turning at top, and 6cm/2¼in for hem at bottom.

Length of embroidery skein for smocking: Buy 6-stranded embroidery skein to smock up the pelmet. Use all 6 strands. You will need ½ skein per material width.

Length of satin ribbon: Use 1.5–3mm/¹⁄₁₆–⅛in-wide double-sided satin ribbon. You will need 3m/3¼yd per material width.

18
OUTLINED, SMOCKED PELMET

With double satin ribbons, contrast bound top and bottom

Again, suitable for all purposes mentioned under no 15 and identical to it, except for the outlining. Two colours of ribbon can be used, and the double ribbon gives an even stronger outline.

CURTAINS

See no 2

PELMET

1 **Width of finished, pleated pelmet:** Width of pelmet board, plus returns at either end.

2 **Width of finished, unpleated pelmet:** As 1 above (width of pelmet board plus returns) × 2.

3 **Unsewn width of pelmet:** As 2 above (width of pelmet board plus returns × 2) plus 8cm/3in for (4cm/1½in) turnings at either side.

4 **Length of smocking tape:** As 2 above (width of pelmet board plus returns × 2) plus 4cm/1½in (2cm/¾in turnings at each end). Use the best-quality commercial smocking tape, 8.5cm/3¼in deep.

5 **Finished drop of pelmet:** Approx. ⅙ total drop of curtains.

6 **Unsewn drop of pelmet:** As 5 above (⅙ total drop of curtains).

7 **Lining quantity:** Width as 3 above; drop as 5 above.

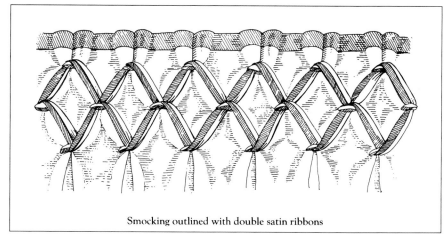

Smocking outlined with double satin ribbons

8 **Interlining quantity:** Width as 2 above; drop as 5 above.

9 **Size of contrast:** Two strips 7cm/2¾in wide and length as in 2, no 15: (width of pelmet board, plus returns at either end, plus 4cm/1½in: 2cm/¾in either end).

10 **Length of embroidery skein for smocking and satin ribbon:** Buy 6-stranded embroidery skein to smock up the pelmet. Use all 6 strands. You will need ½ skein per material width. Then use 3mm/⅛in-wide double-sided satin ribbon: you will need 3m/3¼yd of each colour per material width.

19
OUTLINED, SMOCKED PELMET

With buttons, and top contrast binding

Again, suitable for all purposes mentioned under no 15. The button detail is particularly eye-catching (and it is easy to find a button-covering service). The outlining can be done in embroidery skein or satin ribbon, the second giving a stronger effect than the first.

See above for full directions.

Unsewn drop of pelmet: Approx ⅙ total drop of curtains, plus 6cm/2¼in for hem at bottom.

Size of contrast: 7cm/2¾in wide and length as in 2, no 15: (width of pelmet board, plus returns at either end, plus 4cm/1½in: 2cm/¾in in either end).

Length of embroidery skein for smocking and outlining: Buy 6-stranded embroidery skein to smock up the pelmet. Use all 6 strands. You will need ½ skein per material width.

Length of satin ribbon: Use 3mm/⅛in-wide double-sided satin ribbon. You will need 3m/3¼yd of each colour per material width.

Buttons: 57 × 12mm/½in self-covering buttons per material width.

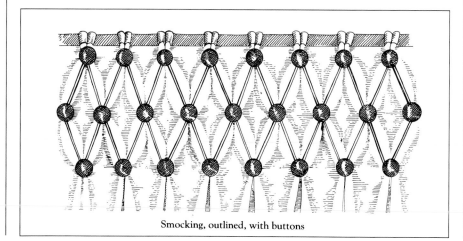

Smocking, outlined, with buttons

20
HONEYCOMB-SMOCKED PELMET

With top contrast binding

Again, suitable for all purposes mentioned under no 15. The honey-comb smocking is just slightly more intricate in appearance.

CURTAINS
See no 2

PELMET

1 **Width of finished, pleated pelmet:** Width of pelmet board, plus returns at either end.

2 **Width of finished, unpleated pelmet:** As 1 above (width of pelmet board plus returns) × 2.

3 **Unsewn width of pelmet:** As 2 above (width of pelmet board plus returns × 2) plus 8cm/3in for (4cm/1½in) turnings at either side.

4 **Length of smocking tape:** As 2 above (width of pelmet board plus returns × 2) plus 4cm/1½in (2cm/¾in turnings at each end). Use the best-quality commercial smocking tape, 8.5cm/3¼in deep.

5 **Finished drop of pelmet:** Approx. ⅙ total drop of curtains.

6 **Unsewn drop of pelmet:** As 5 above (⅙ total drop of curtains) plus 6cm/2¼in for hem at bottom.

7 **Lining quantity:** Width as 3 above; drop as 5 above less 4.5cm/1¾in turn-up in main material, at back.

8 **Interlining quantity:** Width as 2 above; drop as 5 above.

9 **Size of contrast:** Length as 2 above (width of pelmet board plus returns × 2) plus 2cm/¾in turnings at each end); width 7cm/2¾in, which gives 1cm/⅜in showing at the top.

10 **Length of embroidery skein for smocking:** Buy 6-stranded embroidery skein to smock up the pelmet after having pulled up the smocking tape. Use all 6 strands. You will need ¾ skein per material width used in the pelmet.

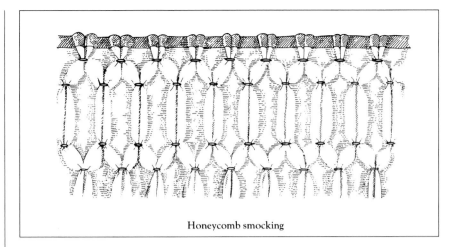

Honeycomb smocking

21
OUTLINED, HONEYCOMB-SMOCKED PELMET

With top contrast binding

Again, suitable for all purposes mentioned under no 15. The honey-comb smocking (see no 20) is made slightly more obvious by the outlining.

See above for full directions

Length of embroidery skein for smocking and outlining: Buy 6-stranded embroidery skein to smock up the pelmet. Use all 6 strands. You will need 1¼ skein per material width. Do not outline this pelmet in ribbon as it is too complicated and would look untidy.

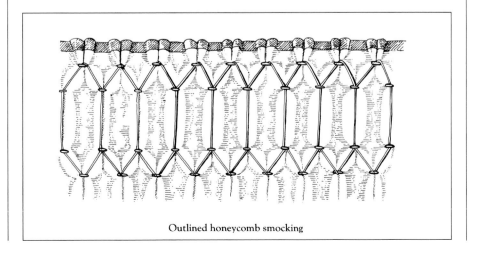

Outlined honeycomb smocking

22
MINIATURE SMOCKED PELMET

Again, suitable for all purposes mentioned under no 15. This design has far greater depth and intricacy than any of the former smocked pelmets.

CURTAINS

See no 2

PELMET

1 Width of finished, pleated pelmet: Width of pelmet board, plus returns at either end.

2 Width of finished, unpleated pelmet: As 1 above (width of pelmet board plus returns) × 2.

3 Unsewn width of pelmet: As 2 above (width of pelmet board plus returns × 2) plus 8cm/3in for (4cm/1½in) turnings at either side.

4 Length of smocking tape: As 2 above (width of pelmet board plus returns × 2) plus 4cm/1½in (2cm/¾in turnings at each end). Use the best-quality commercial smocking tape, 8.5cm/3¼in deep.

5 Finished drop of pelmet: Approx. ⅙ total drop of curtains.

6 Unsewn drop of pelmet: As 5 above (⅙ total drop of curtains) plus 11cm/4¼in: 5cm/2in for turning at top plus 6cm/2¼in for hem at bottom.

7 Lining quantity: Width as 3 above; drop as 5 above less 4.5cm/1¾in turn-up in main material, at back.

8 Interlining quantity: Width as 2 above; drop as 5 above.

9 Length of embroidery skein for smocking: Buy 6-stranded embroidery skein to smock up the pelmet after having pulled up the smocking tape. Use all 6 strands. You will need 1 skein per material width used in the pelmet.

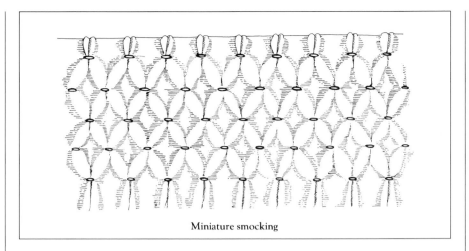

Miniature smocking

23
OUTLINED, MINIATURE SMOCKED PELMET

Again, suitable for all purposes mentioned under no 15. The same as no 22, but outlined. The effect is sensational.

See no 22 for full directions.

Unsewn drop of pelmet: Approx ⅙ total drop of curtains, plus 11cm/4¼in: 5cm/2in for turning at top plus 6cm/2¼in for hem at bottom.

Length of embroidery skein for smocking and outlining: Buy 6-stranded embroidery skein to smock up the pelmet. Use all 6 strands. You will need 2½ skeins per material width.

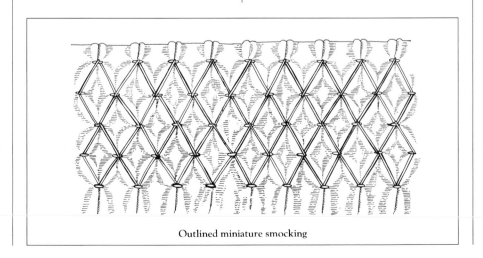

Outlined miniature smocking

24
DOUBLE-DEPTH SMOCKED PELMET

With set-on fringing and top contrast binding

Again, suitable for all purposes mentioned under no 15, but this heading is particularly suitable when dealing with a window whose height can take a much deeper drop. This pelmet has huge depth of character – a wonderful effect.

CURTAINS

See no 2

PELMET

1 **Width of finished, pleated pelmet:** Width of pelmet board, plus returns at either end.

2 **Width of finished, unpleated pelmet:** As 1 above (width of pelmet board plus returns) × 2.

3 **Unsewn width of pelmet:** As 2 above (width of pelmet board plus returns × 2) plus 8cm/3in for (4cm/1½in) turnings at either side.

4 **Length of smocking tape:** As 2 above (width of pelmet board plus returns × 2) plus 4cm/1½in (2cm/¾in turnings at each end). Use 15cm/6in-deep pencil-pleat tape. Machine along top, bottom, sides and middle of tape.

5 **Finished drop of pelmet:** Approx ⅙ total drop of curtains.

6 **Unsewn drop of pelmet:** As 5 above (approx. ⅙ total drop of curtains), plus 6cm/2¼in for hem at bottom.

7 **Lining quantity:** Width as 3 above; drop as 5 above less 4.5cm/1¾in due to hem turn-up in main material, at back.

8 **Interlining quantity:** Width as 2 above; drop as 5 above.

9 **Size of contrast:** Length as 4 above (width of pelmet board, plus returns at either end × 2, plus 2cm/¾in turnings at each end); width 7cm/2¾in, which gives 1cm/⅜in showing at the top.

10 **Length of fringe:** As 4 above.

11 **Length of embroidery skein for smocking:** Buy 6-stranded embroidery skein to smock up the pelmet. Use all 6 strands. You will need 2 skeins per material width.

25
OUTLINED DOUBLE-DEPTH SMOCKED PELMET

With top contrast binding

Again, suitable for all purposes mentioned under No 24, but the outlining doubles the impact and is well worth the little extra effort.

See no 24 for full directions.

Length of embroidery skein for smocking and outlining: Buy 6-stranded embroidery skein to smock up the pelmet. Use all 6 strands. You will need 3 skeins per material width.

26
GATHERED SKIRT ON BUCKRAM BAND

With piping, and contrast-bound skirt

A charming pelmet, versatile and suitable for any reception room, bedroom or bathroom. It has a far more reticent character than any other hand-made headings, and has a lovely old-fashioned air about it.

CURTAINS

See no 2

PELMET

1 **Width of finished pelmet:** Width of pelmet board, plus returns at either end.

2 **Unsewn width of pelmet:**

Band: As 1 above (width of pelmet board plus returns) plus 8cm/3in for (4cm/1½in) turnings at either side.

Skirt: As 1 above (width of pelmet board plus returns) × 2.5 plus 8cm/3in for (4cm/1½in) turnings at either side.

3 **Length of fusible buckram for band:** As 1 above (width of pelmet board plus returns).

4 **Finished drop of pelmet:** Approx. ⅛ to ⅙ total drop of curtains.

5 **Unsewn drop of pelmet:**

Band: 12cm/4¾in: 10cm/4in plus 2cm/¾in for seams: 1cm/⅜in at both top and bottom.

Skirt: anything more than 20cm/8in, plus 2cm/¾in: 1cm/⅜in seam allowance at both top and bottom. It must never be less than double the band – preferably a little more.

6 **Lining quantity:**

Band: Width as 1 above; drop as 5 above.

Skirt: Width as 2 above; drop anything more than 20cm/8in, less 4.5cm/1¾in (to accommodate turn-up of contrast) at the hem.

7 **Interlining quantity:**

Band: Width as 1 above; drop 10cm/4in.

Skirt: Not interlined.

8 **Piping:** See no 106.

9 **Skirt contrast:** Total width of skirt × 7cm/2¾in.

27
GATHERED SKIRT ON PADDED, RUCHED BAND

With piping and contrast-bound skirt

The ruching in this pelmet band, stuffed with interlining for a padded look, has a striking, three-dimensional character that adds power and strength to the pelmet as a whole. It is essential to use hard buckram to stiffen the heavy top of this pelmet; fusible buckram is too weak.

CURTAINS
See no 2

PELMET

1 Width of finished pelmet: Width of pelmet board, plus returns at either end.

2 Unsewn width of pelmet:

Ruched band: As 1 above (width of pelmet board plus returns) × 3, plus 8cm/3in for (4cm/1½in) turnings at either side.

Skirt: As 1 above (width of pelmet board plus returns) × 2.5 plus 8cm/3in for (4cm/1½in) turnings at either side.

3 Length of hard buckram: As 1 above (width of pelmet board plus returns).

4 Finished drop of pelmet: Approx. ⅙ total drop of curtains.

5 Unsewn drop of pelmet:

Band: 14cm/5½in: 12cm/4¾in plus 2cm/¾in for seams: 1cm/⅛in at top and bottom.

Skirt: At least double band size (depending on 4 above), plus 2cm/¾in: 1cm/⅜in seam allowance at top and bottom.

6 Lining quantity:

Band: Width as 1 above; drop as 5 above.

Skirt: Width as 2 above; drop anything more than 24cm/9½in, less 4.5cm/1¾in due to hem turn-up in contrast material, at back.

7 Piping: Two lengths. See no 106.

8 Skirt contrast: Total width of skirt × 7cm/2¾in.

28
SPACED BOX PLEATS ON BUCKRAM BAND

With contrast piping and inset fan-edge trim

A tailored, organised pelmet which has a natural masculine air about it. It is highly successful in many reception rooms, but possibly a little too hard looking for a bedroom, with the exception of a dressing room or a boy's bedroom where it would be highly suitable. It would also look good in a bathroom.

CURTAINS

See no 2

PELMET

1 **Width of finished pelmet:** Width of pelmet board, plus returns at either end.

2 **Width of finished, unpleated pelmet:**

Band: As 1 above (width of pelmet board plus returns).

Skirt: As 1 above (width of pelmet board plus returns) × 2.5.

3 **Unsewn width of pelmet:**

Band: As 1 above plus 8cm/3in for (4cm/1½in) turnings at either side.

Skirt: As 2 above plus 8cm/3in for (4cm/1½in) turnings at either side.

4 **Length of fusible buckram for band:** As 1 above: width of pelmet board plus returns.

5 **Finished drop of pelmet:** Approx. ⅙ total drop of curtains.

6 **Unsewn drop of pelmet:**

Band: 14cm/5½in: 12cm/4¾in plus 2cm/¾in for seams: 1cm/⅜in at top and bottom.

Skirt: At least double band size (depending on 5 above), plus 2cm/¾in for seams: 1cm/⅜in at top and bottom. Cut an additional strip the same length as cut skirt but 7cm/2¾in wide for the hem of the pelmet where the trim in to be inset.

7 **Lining quantity:**

Band: Width as 3 above; drop as 6 above.

Skirt: Width as 3 above; drop as 6 above less 4.5cm/1¾in due to hem turn-up in main material, at back.

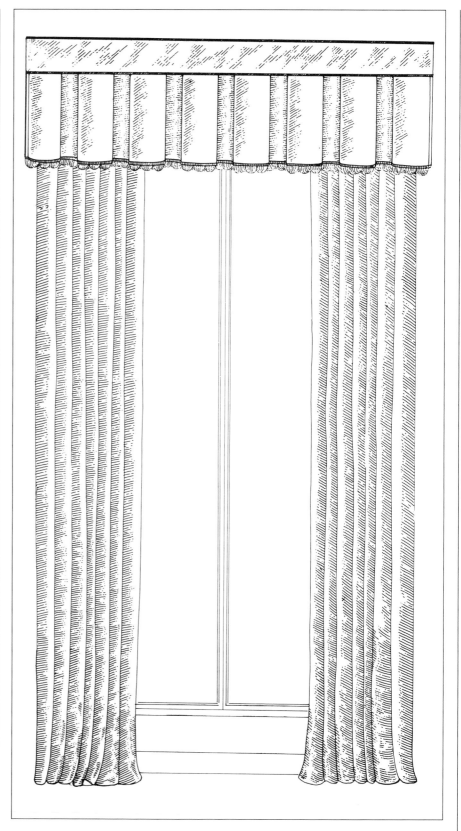

8 **Interlining quantity:**

Band: Width as 2 above; drop 14cm/5½in.

Skirt: Not interlined.

9 **Contrast piping:** Two lengths. See no 106.

10 **Length of fan-edge trim:** As 2, Skirt, above.

29
BOX PLEATS ON A BUCKRAM BAND

With coloured slashes and inset fan-edge trim

See no 27 for description. Here, the contrast slashes give an added dimension and extra depth to the pelmet.

CURTAINS
See no 2

PELMET

1 **Width of finished pelmet:** Width of pelmet board, plus returns at either end.

2 **Width of finished, unpleated pelmet:**

Band: As 1 above (width of pelmet board plus returns).

Skirt: As 1 above (width of pelmet board plus returns) × 3.

3 **Unsewn width of pelmet:**

Band: As 1 above plus 8cm/3in for (4cm/1½in) turnings at either side.

Skirt: As 2 above plus 8cm/3in for (4cm/1½in) turnings at either side.

4 **Length of fusible buckram for band:** As 1 above (width of pelmet board plus returns).

5 **Finished drop of pelmet:** Approx. ⅙ total drop of curtains.

6 **Unsewn drop of pelmet:**

Band: 14cm/5½in: 12cm/4¾in plus 2cm/¾in for seams: 1cm/⅜in at top and bottom.

Skirt: At least double band size (depending on 4 above), plus 2cm/¾in: 1cm/⅜in seam allowance at top and bottom. Cut an additional strip the same length as cut skirt but 7cm/2¾in wide for the hem of the pelmet where the trim in to be inset.

7 **Lining quantity:**

Band: Width as 3 above; drop as 6 above.

Skirt: Width as 2 above; drop double band size less 4.5cm/1¾in due to hem turn-up in main material, at back.

8 **Interlining quantity:**

Band: Width as 1 above; drop 14cm/5½in.

Skirt: Not interlined.

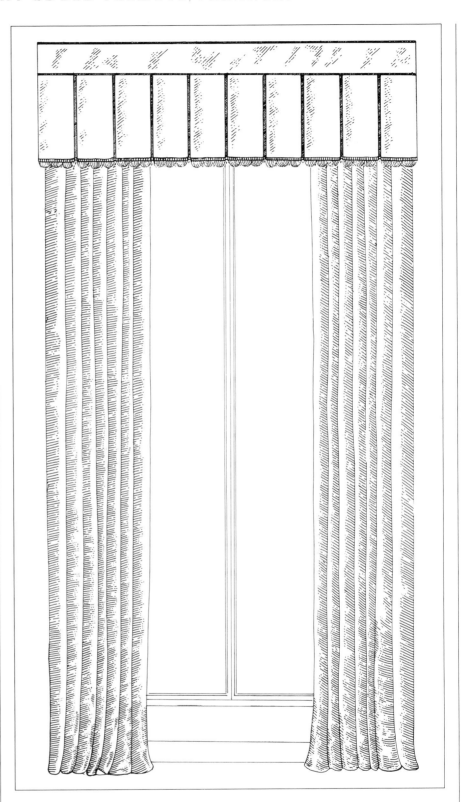

9 **Contrast piping:** Two lengths. See no 106.

10 **Length of fan edge trim:** As 2, Skirt, above.

11 **Coloured slashes:** Cut as many as there will be pleats, minus 1. Same length as unsewn skirt × 9cm wide (2cm allowed for 1cm turnings either side). Before pleating, the slashes are placed where each pleat will fall and the side turnings top stitched, in position, onto the skirt material. The raw edges top and bottom are sewn into the skirt seams.

30

DIAMOND, BUTTONED PELMET

With spaced box pleats

Although this pelmet involves box pleats, here they are made very narrow (4.5–5.5cm/1¾–2¼in) which gives the pelmet a more subtle look than wide box pleats. The heading is good for very shallow drops of pelmet, when a small drop is essential. It also looks good on a larger drop, and the diamond-buttoned detail gives it a frivolous quality, while retaining its geometric look.

This pelmet can never be interlined.

CURTAINS

See no 2

PELMET

1 Width of finished, pleated pelmet: Width of pelmet board, plus returns at either end.

2 Width of finished, unpleated pelmet: As 1 above (width of pelmet board plus returns) × 2.5.

3 Unsewn width of pelmet: As 2 above (width of pelmet board plus returns × 2.5) plus 8cm/3in for (4cm/1½in) turnings at either side.

4 Finished drop of pelmet: Approx. ⅙ total drop of curtains.

5 Unsewn drop of pelmet: As 4 above, plus 11cm/4¼in: 5cm/2in turning at top and 6cm/2¼in for hem at bottom.

6 Lining quantity: Width as 3 above; drop as 4 above (⅙ total drop) minus 5cm/2in.

7 Buttons: 15mm wide: 1 per pleat, covered in contrast colour.

Variation: Contrast bind the edges of the pelmet so that there is 1cm/⅜in of colour showing top and bottom. This gives a sensational look. Cut two 7cm/2¾in strips for both top and bottom, the same length as 3 above.

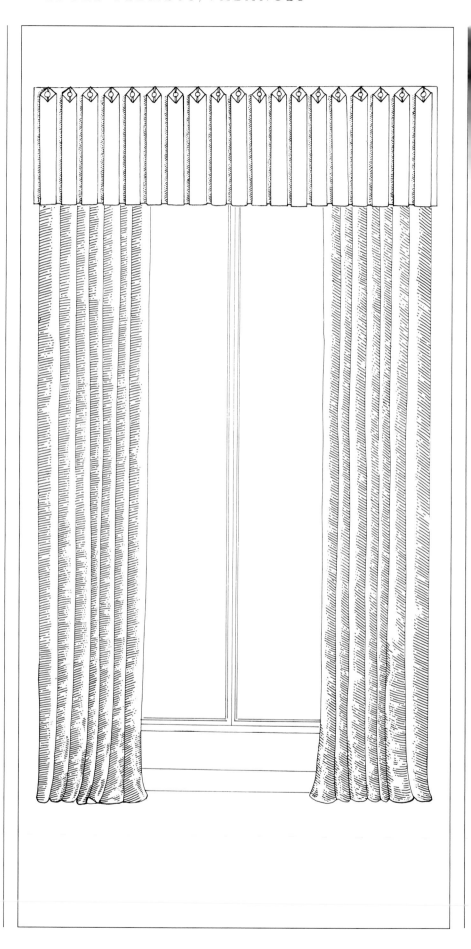

31

DIAMOND, BUTTONED PELMET

With close box pleats

See no 30 for details. Here, the pleats are placed close together, giving a denser look. Consequently, this pelmet uses a greater quantity of material.

CURTAINS

See no 2

PELMET

1 Width of finished, pleated pelmet: Width of pelmet board, plus returns at either end.

2 Width of finished, unpleated pelmet: As 1 above (width of pelmet board plus returns) × 3.

3 Unsewn width of pelmet: As 2 above (width of pelmet board plus returns × 3) plus 8cm/3in for (4cm/1½in) turnings at either side.

4 Finished drop of pelmet: Approx. ⅙ total drop of curtains.

5 Unsewn drop of pelmet: As 4 above, plus 11cm/4¼in: 5cm/2in turning at top and 6cm/2¼in for hem at bottom.

6 Lining quantity: Width as 3 above; drop as 4 above (⅙ total drop) minus 5cm/2in.

7 Buttons: 15mm wide; 1 per pleat, covered in contrast colour.

Variation: Contrast bind the edges of the pelmet so that there is 1cm/⅜in of colour showing top and bottom. See no 30.

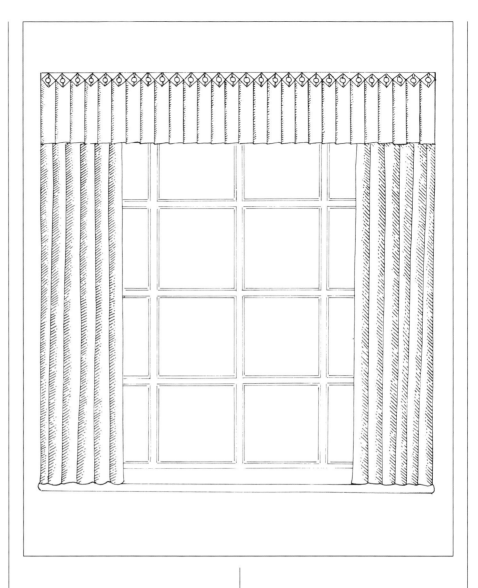

32
STAND-UP, GATHERED PELMET

With a contrast plait

An extremely pretty pelmet for either bedrooms or reception rooms. With a 4cm/1½in stand-up at the top of the pelmet, at least this distance is needed in ceiling clearance.

This pelmet is created by gathering the material directly onto Velcro. It is not only a beautiful effect, but the Velcro is fixed on very easily. It is slightly easier to make without using any interlining, but any used should be very light.

CURTAINS
See no 2

PELMET

1 **Width of finished, pleated pelmet:** Width of pelmet board, plus returns at either end.

2 **Width of finished, unpleated pelmet:** As 1 above (width of pelmet board plus returns) × 3.

3 **Unsewn width of pelmet:** As 2 above (width of pelmet board plus returns × 3) plus 8cm/3in for (4cm/1½in) turnings at either side.

4 **Length of Velcro:** As 1 above (width of pelmet board plus returns).

5 **Finished drop of pelmet:** Approx. ⅙ total drop of curtains, plus 4cm/1½in stand-up above the pelmet board.

6 **Unsewn drop of pelmet:** As 5 above (⅙ total drop plus 4cm/1½in) plus another 17cm/6¾in: 6cm/2¼in for hem, and 11cm/4¼in for stand-up (doubled over and down behind the Velcro).

7 **Lining quantity:** Width as 3 above; drop as 6 above minus 9cm/3½in.

8 **Size of plait:** 2cm/¾in wide once plaited up. The 3 strips should be 25% longer than 1 above, as length is lost in the plaiting process. Cut 3 strips of material 6cm/2¼in wide, and interlining just a little narrower. Put interlining on wrong side of material and fold both over lengthways with wrong sides together. Machine stitch down raw edges with a 1cm/⅜in seam. Put the seam in the centre back of each strip before plaiting up; when

the plait is finished the seams will not be visible at the back of the plait.

Variation: Substitute a caterpillar band (see no 74) for the plait. It should be 2cm/¾in wide, once ruched up.

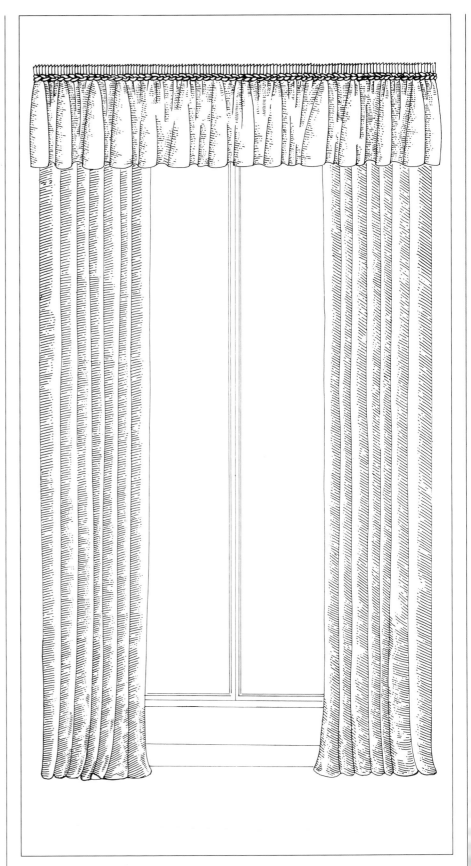

33
GOBLET-PLEATED PELMET

With top and bottom contrast binding, and a toy rabbit in each pleat.

A delightful pelmet for a children's room or a playroom. The rabbits look adorable, with their tall ears balancing the proportions of the pelmet as a whole. It is also a versatile window treatment, as when the child grows up the rabbits can be removed, leaving plain goblets which can be buttoned, or trimmed with a square of contrast colour 'exploding' out of each pleat (like a handkerchief in the breast pocket of a suit).

CURTAINS
See no 2

PELMET

1 Width of finished, pleated pelmet: Width of pelmet board, plus returns at either end.

2 Width of finished, unpleated pelmet: Width of pelmet board × 2.5 then add returns at either end. (The returns are not pleated.)

3 Unsewn width of pelmet: As 2 above (width of pelmet board × 2.5 plus returns) plus 8cm/3in for (4cm/1½in) turnings at either side.

4 Length of buckram: As 2 above (width of pelmet board × 2.5 plus returns).

5 Finished drop of pelmet: Approx. ⅙ total drop of curtains.

6 Unsewn drop of pelmet: As 5 above (⅙ total drop).

7 Lining quantity: Width as 3 above; drop as 6 above minus 4.5cm/1¾in due to hem turn-up in main material, at back.

8 Interling quantity: Width as 2 above; drop as 5 above.

9 Size of contrast: Cut two strips length as 3 above × 7cm/2¾in wide.

10 Special features: One rabbit, approx 8cm/3¼in high, per pleat. It should sit up to its armpits in the pleat. Stitch in, as otherwise child might remove.

Variation: Substitute similar sized teddy bears instead of rabbits.

34

CAUGHT-UP PELMET

With contrast piping, contrast-bound set-on frill and flower rosettes

A sensational pelmet, soft and natural, with no part of it looking tailored or highly organised. It suits a tall window, where the total drop is not less than 2.4m/8ft and the width is not less than 1.25m/4ft.

CURTAINS

See no 2

PELMET

1 **Width of finished pelmet:** Width of pelmet board, plus returns at either end.

2 **Unsewn width of pelmet:**

Band: As 1 above (width of pelmet board plus returns) plus 8cm/3in for (4cm/1½in) turnings at either side.

Skirt: As 1 above × 2.5 plus 8cm/3in for (4cm/1½in) turnings at either side.

3 **Length of fusible buckram for band:** As 1 above (pelmet board plus returns).

4 **Finished drop of pelmet:** Approx. ⅕ total drop of curtains.

5 **Unsewn drop of pelmet:**

Band: 15cm/6in: 12cm/4¾in, plus 1.5cm/⅝in seam allowance top and bottom.

Skirt: 67cm/26in: 60cm/23½in looks good for finished length, plus 7cm/2¾in: 1cm/⅜in seam allowance for the top plus 6cm/2¼in turning for the hem.

6 **Lining quantity:**
Band: Width as 1 above; drop as 5 above.

Skirt: Width as 2 above, drop 63cm/25in.

7 **Interlining quantity:**
Band: Width as 1 above; drop 12cm/4¾in.

Skirt: Interlined with dommette only, never bump.

8 **Contrast piping:** See no 106.

9 **Frill:** See no 105.

10 **Flower rosettes:** See no 86.

35
CONTINUOUS CURVES PELMET

With parallel lines and a double, inset, permanent-pleated frill

One of the most useful and versatile pelmets to know about. It looks good in many situations including tall (but not too slim) windows, a bay, or very wide, straight windows. It is very economical on fabric.

It is essential that the pelmet is both interlined and that the edge is trimmed in contrast which accentuates the inherent shape of the pelmet. The specifications below give quantities for a double frill, with the longer part in a contrast colour. The contrast lines at the top are striking, but not essential.

CURTAINS
See no 2

PELMET

1 Width of finished, pleated pelmet: Width of pelmet board, plus returns at either end.

2 Width of finished, flat pelmet: As 1 above (width of pelmet board plus returns) × 1.5.

3 Width of unsewn pelmet: As 2 above (width of pelmet board plus returns × 1.5) plus 8cm/3in for (4cm/1½in) turnings at either side.

4 Length of fusible buckram: As 2 above (width of pelmet board plus returns × 1.5).

5 Finished drop of pelmet: Approx. ⅙ total drop of curtains (but it curves up and down).

6 Unsewn drop of pelmet: As 5 above plus 11cm/4¼in: 1cm/⅜in seam allowance at hem, plus 10cm/4in turndown over fusible buckram at top.

7 Size of contrast:

Top line: When sewn, 1cm/⅜in showing; material needed 7cm/2¾in × 2 above (width of pelmet board plus returns × 1.5).

Lower line: When sewn 1cm/⅜in showing; material needed 3cm/1¼in × 2 above (pelmet board plus returns × 1.5).

8 Lining quantity: Width as 3 above; drop as 5 above plus 1cm/⅜ seam allowance.

9 Length of flat, ungathered frills: Length of the continuous curving once cut out × a further 2.5 for gathering the frill. (Easiest way to measure is to fold pelmet in 4, measure lower curving edge and multiply × 4.)

10 Drop of unsewn top frill (main material, see no 104): 6.5cm/2½in (including seam allowance of 1cm/⅜in).

11 Width of unsewn underfrill (contrast): 7.5cm/3in (including seam allowance of 1cm/⅜in).

Variation: contrast bound on top only, and a set-on frill that is contrast bound top and bottom (see no 105).

36
ARCHED PELMET WITH FRENCH PLEATS

With top contrast binding and bullion fringe

This pelmet is most suitable for a tall, slim window that faces in any direction. It also looks good on a wide window, as long as it has a reasonable amount of height. Never consider it for a low-ceilinged room, especially if it is north or east facing as the pelmet blocks out too much natural light.

CURTAINS
See no 2

PELMET

1 **Width of finished, pleated pelmet:** Width of pelmet board, plus returns at either end.

2 **Width of finished, unpleated pelmet:** Width of pelmet board × 2.5, then add on returns at either end. (The returns are not pleated.)

3 **Width of unsewn pelmet:** As 2 above (width of pelmet board × 2.5, plus returns) plus 8cm/3in for (4cm/1½in) turnings at either side.

4 **Length of fusible buckram:** As 2 above (width of pelmet board × 2.5, plus returns).

5 **Finished drop of pelmet in centre:** Approx. ⅙ total drop of curtains, plus bullion fringe.

6 **Finished drop of pelmet at sides:** Approx. ⅓ to ¼ total drop of curtains, plus bullion fringe. Remember to allow for pattern repeats, if the material is patterned.

7 **Unsewn drop of pelmet (at lowest point):** As 6 above, plus 16cm/6¼in: 1cm/⅜in seam allowance at bottom and 15cm/6in turn-down at top.

8 **Lining quantity:** Width as 3 above; drop as 6 above plus 1cm/⅜in seam allowance at bottom only.

9 **Interlining quantity:** Width as 2 above; drop as 6 above.

10 **Size of contrast showing at top of pelmet:** When sewn 1cm/⅜in; material

needed 7cm/2¾in × 2 above (width of pelmet board, × 2.5, plus returns).

11 **Length of bullion fringing (10–12cm/4–4¾in wide):** As 2 above (width of pelmet board × 2.5, plus returns) plus 12% for curve.

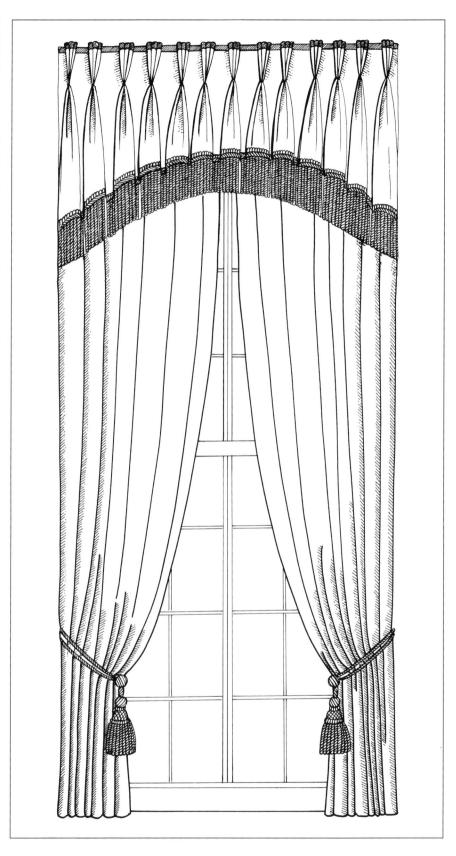

37
SERPENT PELMET WITH FRENCH PLEATS

With top contrast binding, buttons and fringe

A very graceful pelmet with elegant lines. It looks particularly beautiful on tall, slim windows, and is disastrous on wide, low windows, but you can get away with it on a wide window if the drop is substantial. You can use virtually any heading as well as French pleats.

Remember that the pelmet's lower edge continues downwards on the pelmet board returns.

CURTAINS

See no 2

PELMET

1 **Width of finished, pleated pelmet:** Width of pelmet board, plus returns at either end.

2 **Width of finished, unpleated pelmet:** Width of pelmet board × 2.5, then add on returns at either end. (The returns are not pleated.)

3 **Width of unsewn pelmet:** As 2 above (width of pelmet board × 2.5, plus returns) plus 8cm/3in for (4cm/1½in) turnings at either side.

4 **Length of fusible buckram:** As 2 above (width of pelmet board × 2.5, plus returns).

5 **Finished drop of pelmet in centre:** At least ¼ total drop of curtains – but can be more.

6 **Finished drop of pelmet at sides:** Approx. ⅓ total drop of curtains.

7 **Unsewn drop of pelmet (at lowest point):** As 6 above, plus 1cm/⅜in seam allowance at bottom.

8 **Lining quantity:** Width as 3 above; drop as 7 above.

9 **Interlining quantity:** Width as 2 above; drop as 6 above.

10 **Size of contrast:** Length as 2 above × 7cm/2¾in wide.

11 **Length of fringing** (8cm/3¼in long

minimum): As length of lower edge of skirt.

12 **Buttons:** One 15mm button per pleat.

Shaped Pelmet Boards

38
CONVEX BOARD FOR PELMET

A pelmet board with a convex shape gives an interesting dimension to a window treatment. It is important to make the curved shape fairly deep, and it must not have any returns – merely continuing the curve until it meets the wall.

The board must be covered on its underside with matching material as this side can be seen easily.

CURTAINS
See no 2

PELMET
Choose any design and hang from edge of board with Velcro.

1 Depth of convex board in centre: 30cm/12in minimum.

2 **Width of board:** Width of window plus 10% housing space allowance beyond each architrave.

3 **Curtain rail:** Must follow curved shape exactly, set approx 8cm/3¼in back from front of board.

39
PELMET ON SHAPED BOARD

With contrast-bound set-on frill and decorative cord

A grand affair for a reception room or even a bedroom, as it can have very pretty lines. Obviously, a good ceiling clearance is needed to carry off such a design.

The pelmet is cut completely straight – not using a template to transfer the shape of the board – so that the lower frilled edge echoes the upper, fixed one. The top of the pelmet is gathered or ruched in two places, and webbing tape is hand sewn on (but stitched at its top edge only). The free edge of the tape goes down the back of the shaped edge of the board to fix the pelmet into place.

It is essential to trim the lower edge with a frill or fringe to enhance the impact of the shape. The decorative cord is hand stitched in place at the lower ruche line.

CURTAINS
See no 2

PELMET

1 **Width of finished, pleated pelmet:** Follow exact curve of top of board, plus returns at either end.

2 **Width of finished, unpleated pelmet:** As 1 above (length of curved top plus returns) × 3.

3 **Width of unsewn pelmet:** As 2 above (width of pelmet board plus returns × 3) plus 8cm/3in for (4cm/1½in) turnings at either side.

4 **Length of 3cm/1¼in-wide webbing tape:** As 1 above (length of curved top plus returns).

5 **Finished drop of pelmet:** Approx. ⅙ total drop of curtains, including set-on frill. Remember to allow for pattern repeats, if the material is patterned.

6 **Unsewn drop of pelmet:** As 4 above (⅙ total drop of curtains) plus 1cm/⅜in turn-over at top (where webbing tape is attached) and 6cm/2¼in for hem.

7 **Lining quantity:** Width as 3 above; drop as 6 above minus 4cm/1½in.

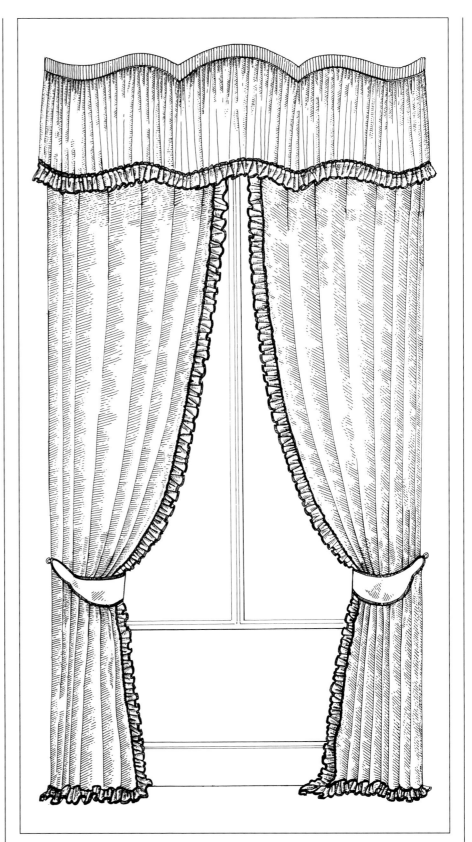

8 **Interlining quantity:** Do not interline.

9 **Length of flat, ungathered frill:** As 2 above (length of curved top plus returns × 3) × a further 2.5 for gathering the frill.

10 **Drop of frill:** See no 105.

11 **Length of decorative rope:** As 1 above.

Swags and Tails

40
RUCHED SWAGS AND TAILS

With inset, piped permanent-pleated frill

This type of swag is very effective to look at and, unlike real, hand-made, tailored swags, is both easy and inexpensive to make. Their sole limitation is that they only work on a certain size of window. For example, a pair of ruched swags look perfect on a window width of between 1–1.2m/ 3ft 3in–4ft, but no wider).

The swags are vertically gathered, not horizontally. If you make them too wide (ie, over 60cm/2ft, their drop can no longer keep in proportion with their width. You can, of course, use three swags on a window whose width is 1.6m/6ft 3in approx., or four swags on a window with a width of 2.4m/8ft (ie, using multiples of 60cm/2ft). The drop of the window should not be less than 2.4m/8ft.

The swags are very easy to make, a bit like an Austrian blind. Use only light interlining, and machine stitch on narrow gathering tape either side of each swag.

CURTAINS
See no 2

SWAGS AND TAILS

1 **Width of finished swag:** Exact width of pelmet board.

2 **Drop of finished swag:** Approx. ⅓ to ⅙ total drop of curtains.

3 **Length of fabric for swag:** Double drop of finished swag, plus 3cm/1¼in for turnings: 1.5cm/⅝in top and bottom.

4 **Width of fabric for swag:** Width of pelmet board plus 3cm/1¼in for seams: 1.5cm/⅝in at either side.

5 **Length of Velcro:** As 1 above: exact width of pelmet board.

6 **Width of finished, pleated tail (at top):** Approx. 37cm/14½in. (This includes 17cm/6¾in for the return.)

7 **Width of flat tail before pleating:** Approx. 90cm/35½in.

8 **Drop of tails (longest section):** Half total height of window (top of pelmet board to carpet).

9 **Drop of tails (shortest section):** Level with lowest edge of swag.

10 **Length of frill before permanent pleating:** 2.5 × lower edge of all 3 items to be trimmed, ie one pair of swags and two tails. See no 104.

11 **Length of piping:** Lower edge of all 3 items to be trimmed, ie one pair of swags and two tails. See no 106.

41
CLASSIC SINGLE SWAG, AND TAILS

With permanent-pleated contrast frill

This classic treatment suits a tall, slim window only – no less than 2.4m/8ft high – and is especially suitable if your house really has high ceilings.

CURTAINS

See no 2

SWAGS AND TAILS

1 **Width of finished swag:** Width of pelmet board, or just a little less.

2 **Drop of finished swag:** Approx. $\frac{1}{6}$ total drop of curtains.

3 **Length of fabric for swag:** Cut at least 2 times the drop of the finished swag (2 above), and sometimes 3.

4 **Width of fabric for swag:** Width of pelmet board plus approx. 50% (The lower edge of the swag is very wide.)

5 **Width of finished, pleated tail (at top):** Approx. 37cm/14½in. (This includes 17cm/6¾in for the return.)

6 **Width of flat tail before pleating:** Approx. 90cm/35½in.

7 **Drop of tails (longest section):** Half total height of window (top of pelmet board to carpet).

8 **Drop of tails (shortest section):** Level with lowest edge of swag.

9 **Length of frill before permanent pleating:** Three times lower edge of all 3 items to be trimmed, ie one swag and two tails. See no 104.

42
SINGLE SWAG WRAPPED OVER A POLE

With asymmetrical tails and set-on fringe

The details for no 41 also apply here. The asymmetrical detail – used as a mirror image – looks particularly good when dressing a pair of windows, or even four.

CURTAINS

See no 2

SWAGS AND TAILS

1 **Width of finished swag:** Exact length of the pole, plus approx. 10% (so that it can both wrap around the pole at both ends).

2 **Drop of finished swag:** ⅕ to ⅙ total drop of curtains.

3 **Length of fabric for swag:** Cut 2 to 3 times the drop of finished swag (2 above). Then cut out a curve at the top of the swag to shape it so that the top 'swags' down effectively below the pole.

4 **Width of fabric for swag:** Exact length of pole, plus approx. 50%. (The lower edge of the swag is very wide.)

5 **Width of finished, pleated tail (at top):** Approx. 37cm/14½in. (This includes 17cm/6¾in for the return.)

6 **Width of flat tail before pleating:** Approx 90 cm/35½in.

7 **Drop of tails:** Half total height of window (top of pole to carpet) for long tail; short tail much less.

8 **Fringe:** Entire length of lower edge of all three items to be trimmed, ie one swag and two tails.

43
PAIR OF SWAGS, AND TAILS

With piped, permanent-pleated trim

Like nos 41 and 42, this type of treatment suits a tall, slim window only – no less than 2.4m/8ft high.

CURTAINS

See no 2

SWAGS AND TAILS

1 **Width of finished swag:** ⅔ exact length of pelmet board.

2 **Drop of finished swag:** ⅕ to ⅙ total drop of curtains.

3 **Length of fabric for swag:** Cut 2 times the drop of finished swag (2 above).

4 **Width of fabric for swag:** ⅔ length of pelmet board, plus approx. 50%. (The lower edge of the swag is very wide.)

5 **Width of finished, pleated tail (at top):** Approx. 37cm/14½in. (This includes 17cm/6¾in for the return.)

6 **Width of flat tail before pleating:** Approx. 90 cm/35½in.

7 **Drop of tails (longest section):** Half total height of window (top of board to carpet).

8 **Drop of tails (shortest section):** Level with lowest edge of swag.

9 **Length of frill before permanent pleating:** 3 times lower edge of all 3 items to be trimmed, ie one swag and two tails. See no 104.

10 **Contrast piping:** Length of lower edge of swags and tails × 4cm/1½in. See no 106.

44
THREE SWAGS, AND TAILS

With central rosette

All that applies to no 41 is relevant here. This treatment is a slightly more subtle look, with more depth than ordinary overlapping swags. It also creates an illusion of being one large swag, caught up with the rosette to reveal another behind, but it does, in fact, consist of three swags.

CURTAINS
See no 2

SWAGS AND TAILS

1 **Width of each finished swag:** Half of exact length of pelmet board.

2 **Drop of finished swag:** ⅕ to ⅙ total drop of curtains.

3 **Length of fabric for swag:** Cut 2 to 2.5 times the drop of finished swag (2 above).

4 **Width of fabric for swag:** Half width of pelmet board plus approx. 50%. (The lower edge of the swag is very wide.)

5 **Width of finished, pleated tail (at top):** Approx. 37cm/14½in. (This includes 17cm/6¾in for the return.)

6 **Width of flat tail before pleating:** Approx. 90 cm/35½in.

7 **Drop of tails (longest section):** Half total height of window (top of pelmet board to carpet).

8 **Drop of tails (shortest section):** Level with lowest edge of swags.

9 **Rosette:** Choux rosette, see no 84.

45
FOUR OVERLAPPING SWAGS, AND TAILS

With fringing and contrast facing

This is a splendid, old-fashioned way of treating a tall, wide window.

Do not ever attempt to overlap real swags around a bay window. This is because they are only vertically gathered and do not have any horizontal fullness. Therefore, they cannot hang straight down and around a curve simultaneously.

CURTAINS

See no 2

SWAGS AND TAILS

1 Width of each finished swag: Approx. ⅓ exact length of pelmet board.

2 Drop of finished swag: ⅕ to ⅙ total drop of curtains.

3 Length of fabric for swag: Cut 2 times the drop of finished swag (2 above).

4 Width of fabric for swag: ⅓ length of pelmet board plus approx. 50%. (The lower edge of the swag is very wide.)

5 Width of finished, pleated tail (at

top): Approx 37cm/14½in. (This includes 17cm/6¾in for the return.)

6 Width of flat tail before pleating: Approx 90 cm/35½in.

7 Drop of tails (longest section): Half total height of window (top of pelmet board to carpet).

8 Drop of tails (shortest section): Level with lowest edge of swags.

9 Fringing quantity: Entire length of lower edge of all 6 items to be trimmed, ie 4 swags and 2 tails.

10 Contrast colour on facing to tails: Cut contrast lining exactly the same size as tail main fabric.

46
CURVING SWAGS

Over Velcro-headed pelmet

A grand affair, on a par with the more usual swags and tails. It is extremely elegant, and the two layers in the pelmet create a detail that is extremely eye-catching. To make best use of it, it is essential to have the back layer in a material that contrasts with the front layer.

Use dommette only as the interlining as bump is too heavy in this situation and would ruin the effect.

CURTAINS
See no 2

VELCRO-HEADED PELMET (BACK LAYER)

1 **Width of finished, gathered pelmet:** Width of pelmet board, plus returns at either end.

2 **Width of finished, flat pelmet:** As 1 above (width of pelmet board plus returns) × 2.5–3.

3 **Length of Velcro:** As 1 above (width of pelmet board plus returns).

4 **Finished drop of pelmet:** Approx ⅙ total drop of curtains.

5 **Unsewn drop of pelmet:** As 4 above (⅙ total drop) plus 18cm/7in: 12cm/4¾in for turning and stand-up at top plus 6cm/2¼in for hem at bottom.

PELMET SWAGS (FRONT LAYER)

1 **Width of each finished swag:** Half the length of pelmet board.

2 **Drop of finished swag:** To fall just below the Velcro-headed pelmet (inclusive of fringe).

3 **Length of fabric for swag:** As 2 above, × 2.

4 **Width of fabric for swag:** As 1 above plus 50%.

5 **Width of finished tail:** Approx. 37cm/14½in.

6 **Width of flat tail before pleating:** Approx. 84cm/33in.

7 **Drop of tail (longest section):** Half total height of window (top of pelmet board to carpet).

8 **Drop of tail (shorter section):** Level with lowest edge of swag.

9 **Fringing quantity:** Same length as lower edge of all four items to be trimmed, ie two swags and two tails.

10 **Special feature:** This tail has five pleats and they are placed on top of each other.

47
THREE OVERLAPPING SWAGS, AND TAILS

Off a piped, ruched band

This is a very lavish, elegant look and even more eye catching than all those previously mentioned because of its somewhat theatrical character. It is also the perfect curtain solution for a bay window with a seat in the window area.

Put a pelmet board across the flat surface at the front of the window recess. Make a huge pair of 'dress' curtains, cut very long and full, and hold them back with tie-backs (see nos 71–80). Use roller or Roman blinds (no 94) to cover the three windows, and finish it off with a matching seat cushion (nos 69–70).

CURTAINS
See no 2

Use three widths of fabric for each curtain.
Add an extra 15cm/6in onto the curtain length so that they 'puddle' on the floor.

SWAGS AND TAILS

1 Width of each finished swag: Approx. ²/₃ exact length of pelmet board.

2 Drop of finished swag: ¹/₅ to ¹/₆ total drop of curtains.

3 Length of fabric for swag: Cut 2 to 3 times the drop of finished swag (2 above).

4 Width of fabric for swag: As length 1 above (²/₃ of pelmet board) plus approx. 50%. (The lower edge of the swag is very wide.)

5 Width of finished, pleated tail (at top): Approx. 37cm/14½in. (This includes 17cm/6¾in for the return.)

6 Width of flat tail before pleating: Approx. 90 cm/35½in.

7 Drop of tails (longest section): Half total height of window (top of pelmet board to carpet).

8 Drop of tails (shortest section): Level with lowest edge of swags.

9 Piped, ruched band, finished size: Exact width of board, plus its returns.

10 Unsewn length of ruched band: As 9 above, × 3.

11 Piping: Two lengths. See no 106.

Hard Buckram Pelmets

48
VARIOUS BUCKRAM PELMETS

Pelmets made with a hard buckram backing can suit any window: small or large, tall and slim, low and wide. You merely scale up or down the buckram shape. They have a charmingly old-fashioned look, and are greatly enhanced by adding some type of braid, edging or fringe.

The pelmet board must have a timber fascia and vertical returns to give this pelmet the necessary support.

Cut this hard buckram (which bears no relation to the narrow, white, fusible buckram) with paper scissors only. It is full of glue, so spray it with water and iron on interlining with a very hot iron, wrapping at least 5cm/2in of interlining around the back. Place the main material over the interlining, folding it over to the back and hand stitching it onto the 'glued' interlining. Back the pelmet with lining material, sewing it to the main material by hand.

CURTAINS
See no 2

PELMET

1 **Width of finished flat pelmet:** Width of pelmet board, plus returns at either end.

2 **Length of Velcro for fastening pelmet onto board:** As 1 above.

3 **Drop of finished pelmet:** Approx ¹/₇ total drop of curtains. (These hard pelmets are slightly shallower than those of soft, pleated or gathered pelmets.)

4 **Unsewn dimensions of pelmet:** Cut main material and interlining to fit desired finished size of hard buckram shape, plus a 5cm/2in turning around all 4 sides.

5 **Size of lining:** Cut to fit desired finished size of hard buckram shape, plus 1.5cm/⅝in turning around all 4 sides.

Bed Valances/Skirts/ Dust Ruffles

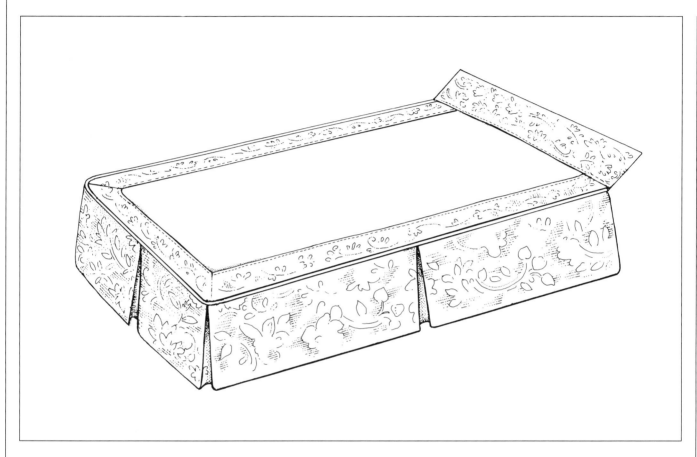

49

KICK-PLEATED BED VALANCE

The simplest type of bed valance to make and the most economical in fabric quantity. It is highly suitable for masculine rooms, but also when other items in the room (such as curtains, pelmets, coronas and dressing tables) are already rather frilled and gathered.

Every bed valance should have a lip, made of main material, so that unsightly lining does not show at the edge of the mattress. It must be piped at the seam where the skirt is attached, for a really professional look. The flap at the head end helps to keep the valance in place under the mattress.

1 **Finished size of valance base:** Exactly the same size as the bed base. Cut from lining material, and border it with a piped lip (see below).

2 **Finished drop of bed valance:** From top edge of bed base to carpet.

3 **Fullness of skirt:** Distance round 3 sides of the bed (excluding the head end) plus 20cm/8in per box pleat. (Four pleats needed for a single bed; 5 pleats needed for a double bed or larger.)

4 **Cutting length for skirt:** As 2 above (top edge of bed base to carpet) plus 7cm/2¾in (1.5cm/⅝in seam allowances top and bottom, and 4cm/1½in turn-up at the lower edge).

5 **Cutting length for skirt lining:** As 2 above: top edge of bed base to carpet, less 1cm/⅜in. (This allows for 1.5cm/⅝in seam allowances top and bottom.)

6 **Finished size of lip:** 12cm/4¾in wide, to run the length of both long sides and along the foot end. Cut from main material.

7 **Finished size of flap at head end:** 20cm/8in × width of bed.

8 **Piping:** Make length same as *outside* lengths of finished lip. See no 106.

50
KICK-PLEATED BED VALANCE

With contrast-bound edge

This valance is exactly the same as no 49, except that it has a 2cm/¾in-wide binding along its lower edge. This gives it a special, extra look, and a little more elegance.

1 **Finished size of valance base:** Exactly the same size as the bed base. Cut from lining material, and border it with a piped lip (see below).

2 **Finished drop of bed valance:** From top edge of bed base to carpet.

3 **Fullness of skirt:** Distance round three sides of the bed (excluding the head end) plus 20cm/8in per box pleat. (Four pleats needed for a single bed; 5 pleats needed for a double bed or larger.)

4 **Cutting length for skirt:** As 2 above (top edge of bed base to carpet) plus 1.5cm/⅝in seam allowance for top. (The lower edge is bound with the contrast.)

5 **Cutting length for skirt lining:** As 2 above (top edge of bed base to carpet) less 2.5cm/1in, as the contrast binding along the lower edge will be turned up 4cm/1½in under the valance skirt as the hem.

6 **Finished size of lip:** 12cm/5in wide, to run the length of both long sides and along the foot end. Cut from main material.

7 **Finished size of flap at head end:** 20cm/8in × width of bed.

8 **Piping:** Cut strip same as *outside* lengths of finished lip. See no 106.

9 **Size of contrast binding:** When sewn 2cm/¾in showing; material needed 9cm/3½in × 3 above.

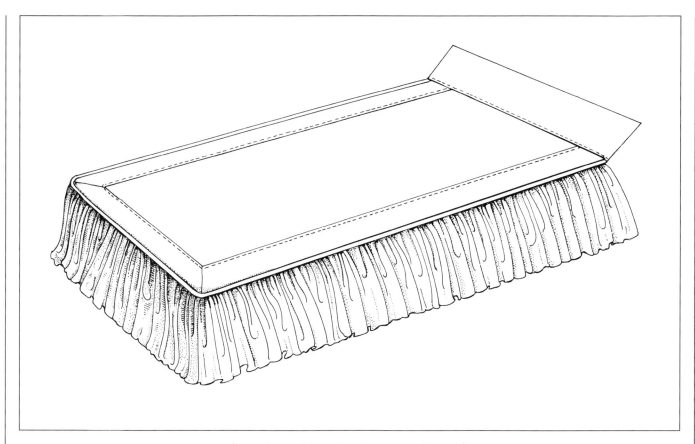

51

GATHERED-SKIRT BED VALANCE

This style of bed valance has a definite feminine character. In addition, its fullness gives it a slightly lavish look. It is excellent in nearly every situation except when you are trying to create a masculine atmosphere in a bedroom, or else when other items in the bedroom are already very gathered and frilled, such as pelmets, a dressing table, round table covers, a corona, or half-tester.

Never interline a bed valance as it must look light and flouncy.

1 **Finished size of valance base:** Exactly the same size as the bed base. Cut from lining material, and border it with a piped lip (see below).

2 **Finished drop of bed valance:** From top edge of bed base to carpet plus 1cm/⅜in which makes the skirt flare out attractively.

3 **Fullness of skirt:** 2.5 times at least, around 3 sides of the bed (excluding the head end).

4 **Cutting length for skirt:** As 2 above (top edge of bed base to carpet, plus 1cm/⅜in) plus 7cm/2¾in (1.5cm/⅝in seam allowances top and bottom, and 4cm/1½in turn-up at the lower edge).

5 **Cutting length for skirt lining:** As 2 above: top edge of bed base to carpet, less 1cm/⅜in. (This allows for 1.5cm/⅝in seam allowances top and bottom.)

6 **Finished size of lip:** 12cm/5in wide, to run the length of both long sides and along the foot end. Cut from main material.

7 **Finished size of flap at head end:** 20cm/8in × width of bed.

8 **Piping:** Cut strip same as *outside* lengths of finished lip. See no 106.

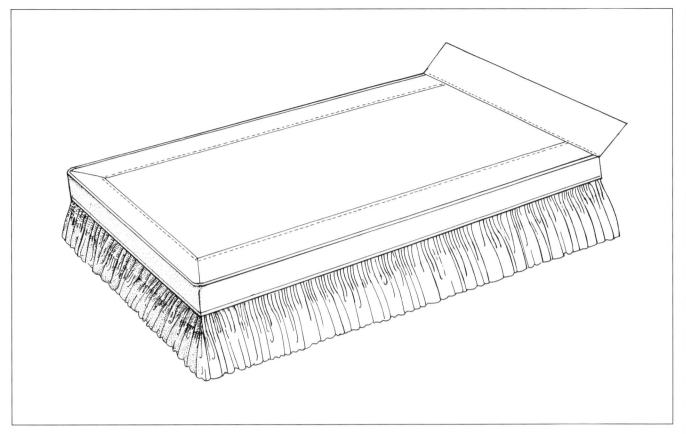

52
GATHERED-SKIRT BED VALANCE

Off a piped band

All that typifies no 51 also applies here, but in addition, this valance is especially suitable for a bed that is higher off the floor than normal (often found with brass or four-poster beds). It also has a slightly more organised look than the plain gathered-skirt valance.

1 **Finished size of valance base:** Exactly the same size as the bed base. Cut from lining material, and border it with a piped lip (see below).

2 **Finished drop of bed valance:** From top edge of bed base to carpet plus 1cm/ ³⁄₈in, which makes the skirt flare out attractively.

3 **Fullness of skirt:** 2.5 times at least around 3 sides of the bed (excluding the head end).

4 **Depth of piped band:** Just under ⅓ of the overall drop of the skirt looks best in terms of proportions, plus 3cm/1¼in for seams. Cut lining for band the same size.

5 **Length of piped band:** Three sides of the bed, plus a total of 4cm/1½in for turnings.

6 **Cutting length for skirt:** As 2 above (top edge of bed base to carpet, plus 1cm/ ³⁄₈in) less the finished depth of the band, plus 7cm/2¾in (1.5cm/⁵⁄₈in seam allowances top and bottom, and 4cm/1½in turn-up at the lower edge).

7 **Cutting length for skirt lining:** Cut 8cm/3¼in less than cut skirt length (not band). (This allows for 1.5cm/⁵⁄₈in seam allowances top and bottom.)

8 **Finished size of lip:** 12cm/5in wide, to run the length of both long sides and along the foot end. Cut from main material.

9 **Finished size of flap at head end:** 20cm/8in × width of bed.

10 **Piping:** Cut two lengths same as *outside* lengths of finished lip. (The band is piped both top and bottom.) See no 106.

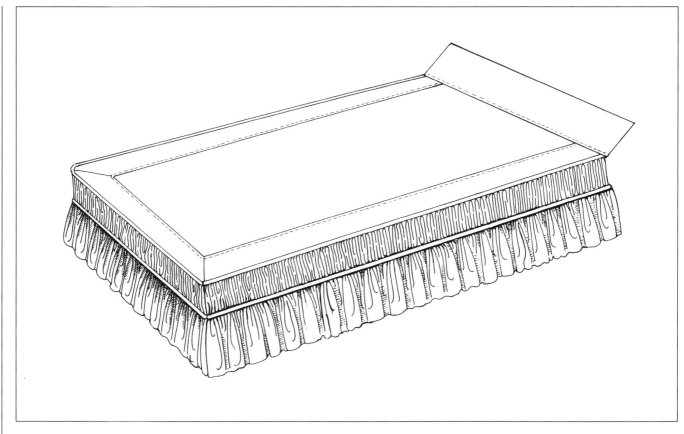

53

GATHERED SKIRT BED VALANCE

Off a piped, ruched band

A valance that is very similar to no 52, except that the piped band is ruched, rather than flat.

1 **Finished size of valance base:** Exactly the same size as the bed base. Cut from lining material, and border it with a piped lip (see below).

2 **Finished drop of bed valance:** From top edge of bed base to carpet plus 1cm/³⁄₈in which makes the skirt flare out attractively.

3 **Fullness of skirt:** 2.5 times at least around 3 sides of the bed (excluding the head end).

4 **Depth of piped, ruched band:** Just under ⅓ of the overall drop of the skirt looks best in terms of proportions, plus 3cm/1¼in for seams. Cut lining for band same size.

5 **Length of piped band:** Three sides of the bed × 3, plus a total of 4cm/1½in for turnings.

6 **Cutting length for skirt:** As 2 above (top edge of bed base to carpet, plus 1cm/³⁄₈in) less the finished depth of the band, plus 7cm/2¾in (1.5cm/⅝in seam allowances top and bottom, and 4cm/1½in turn-up at the lower edge).

7 **Cutting length for skirt lining:** Cut 8cm/3¼in less than cut skirt length (not band). (This allows for 1.5cm/⅝in seam allowances top and bottom.)

8 **Finished size of lip:** 12cm/5in wide, to run the length of both long sides and along the foot end. Cut from main material.

9 **Finished size of flap at head end:** 20cm/8in × width of bed.

10 **Piping:** Cut two strips same as *outside* lengths of finished lip. (The band is piped on both sides.) See no 105.

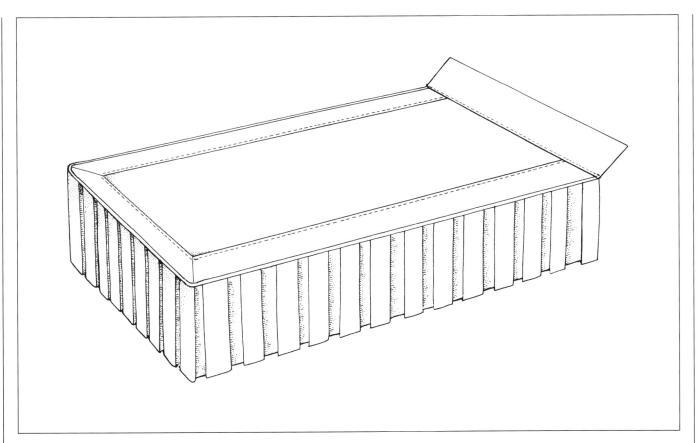

54
SPACED BOX-PLEATED BED VALANCE

This valance achieves the same sort of effect as a kick-pleated valance, but it is not as economical in fabric as 2.5 times around three sides of the bed is needed. It has a particularly tailored and organised character, and is slightly old-fashioned looking which is very much part of its charm.

The pleats should be about 9cm/ 3½in wide, with a 5cm/2in gap between each one.

1 **Finished size of valance base:** Exactly the same size as the bed base. Cut from lining material, and border it with a piped lip (see below).

2 **Finished drop of bed valance:** From top edge of bed base to carpet.

3 **Fullness of skirt:** 2.5 times around three sides of the bed (excluding the head end).

4 **Cutting length for skirt:** As 2 above (top edge of bed base to carpet) plus 7cm/ 2¾in (1.5cm/⅝in seam allowances top and bottom, and 4cm/1½in turn-up at the lower edge).

5 **Cutting length for skirt lining:** As 2 above: top edge of bed base to carpet, less 1cm/⅜in. (This allows for 1.5cm/⅝in seam allowances top and bottom.)

6 **Finished size of lip:** 12cm/5in wide, to run the length of both long sides and along the foot end. Cut from main material.

7 **Finished size of flap at head end:** 20cm/8in × width of bed.

8 **Piping:** Cut strip same as *outside* lengths of finished lip. See no 106.

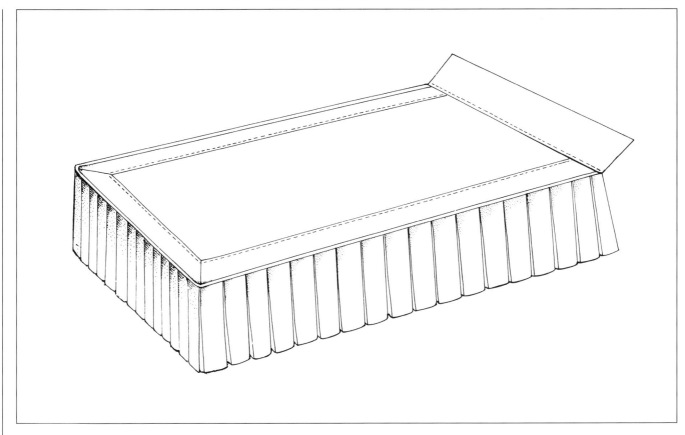

55

CLOSE BOX-PLEATED VALANCE

A similar style to no 54, except that the box pleats (approx 9–12cm/3½–5in wide) are placed together without any spacing. This uses more fabric, but results in a very pleasing, geometric look.

1 **Finished size of valance base:** Exactly the same size as the bed base. Cut from lining material, and border it with a piped lip (see below).

2 **Finished drop of bed valance:** From top edge of bed base to carpet.

3 **Fullness of skirt:** Three times around 3 sides of the bed (excluding the head end).

4 **Cutting length for skirt:** As 2 above (top edge of bed base to carpet) plus 7cm/2¼in (1.5cm/⅝in seam allowances top and bottom, and 4cm/1½in turn-up at the lower edge).

5 **Cutting length for skirt lining:** As 2 above: top edge of bed base to carpet, less 1cm/⅜in. (This allows for 1.5cm/⅝in seam allowances top and bottom.)

6 **Finished size of lip:** 12cm/5in wide, to run the length of both long sides and along the foot end. Cut from main material.

7 **Finished size of flap at head end:** 20cm/8in × width of bed.

8 **Piping:** Cut strip same as *outside* lengths of finished lip. See no 106.

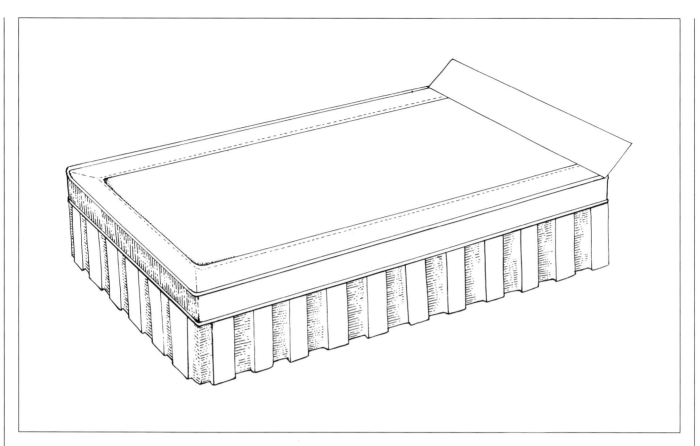

56

SPACED BOX-
PLEATED BED
VALANCE

Off a piped band

This is very similar to no 54, except that the pleats drop from a piped band. This valance is especially suitable for a bed that is higher off the floor than normal (often found with brass or four-poster beds).

The pleats should be about 9cm/ 3½in wide, with a 5cm/2in gap between each one.

1 Finished size of valance base: Exactly the same size as the bed base. Cut from lining material, and border it with a piped lip (see below).

2 Finished drop of bed valance: From top edge of bed base to carpet.

3 Fullness of skirt: 2.5 times around 3 sides of the bed (excluding the head end).

4 Depth of piped band: No more than ⅓ of the overall drop of the skirt, plus 3cm/1¼in for seams.

5 Length of piped band: Three sides of the bed, plus a total of 4cm/1½in for turnings.

6 Cutting length for skirt: As 2 above (top edge of bed base to carpet) less the finished depth of the band, plus 7cm/ 2¾in (1.5cm/⅝in seam allowances top and bottom, and 4cm/1½in turn-up at the lower edge).

7 Cutting length for skirt lining: Cut 8cm/3¼in less than cut skirt length (not band). (This allows for 1.5cm/⅝in seam allowances top and bottom.)

8 Finished size of lip: 12cm/5in wide, to run the length of both long sides and along the foot end. Cut from main material.

9 Finished size of flap at head end: 20cm/8in × width of bed.

10 Piping: Cut two strips same as *outside* lengths of finished lip. (The band is piped on both sides.) See no 106.

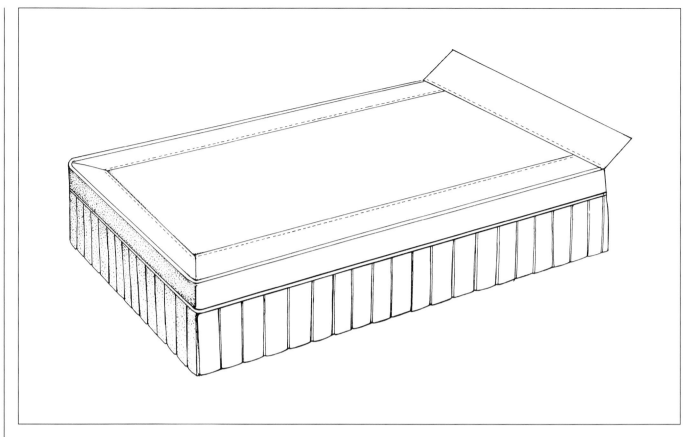

57

CLOSE BOX-PLEATED BED VALANCE

Off a piped band

This uses the type of pleats (approx 9–12cm/3½–5in wide) found on no 55, but like no 56, is especially suitable for a bed that is higher off the floor than normal.

1 **Finished size of valance base:** Exactly the same size as the bed base. Cut from lining material, and border it with a piped lip (see below).

2 **Finished drop of bed valance:** From top edge of bed base to carpet.

3 **Fullness of skirt:** Three times around 3 sides of the bed (excluding the head end).

4 **Depth of piped band:** No more than ⅓ of the overall drop of the skirt, plus 3cm/1¼in for seams.

5 **Length of piped band:** Three sides of the bed, plus a total of 4cm/1½in for turnings.

6 **Cutting length for skirt:** As 2 above (top edge of bed base to carpet) less the finished depth of the band, plus 7cm/2¾in (1.5cm/⅝in seam allowances top and bottom, and 4cm/1½in turn-up at the lower edge).

7 **Cutting length for skirt lining:** Cut 8cm/3¼in less than cut skirt length (not band). (This allows for 1.5cm/⅝in seam allowances top and bottom.)

8 **Finished size of lip:** 12cm/5in wide, to run the length of both long sides and along the foot end. Cut from main material.

9 **Finished size of flap at head end:** 20cm/8in × width of bed.

10 **Piping:** Cut two strips same as *outside* lengths of finished lip. (The band is piped on both sides.) See no 106.

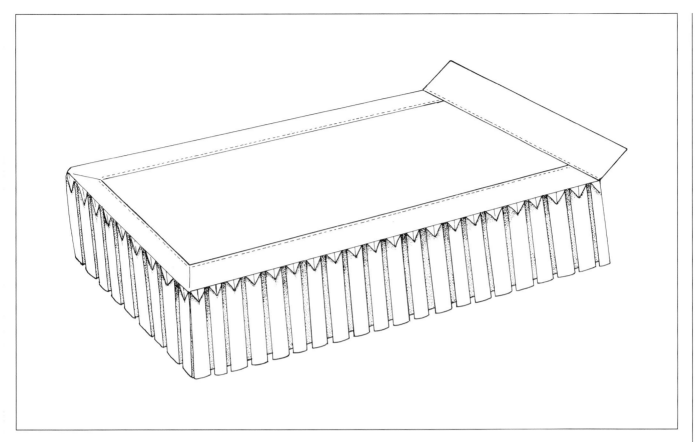

58
BOX-PLEATED VALANCE

With triangular points

A valance with a contemporary look and a geometric character. It is like a spaced box-pleated valance, but with a real difference. It would look particularly fitting in a room where the triangular element was echoed in a diamond-smocked and buttoned window pelmet.

It is extravagant on material since the only way to make it is to use the main material for both back and front of the entire skirt (instead of using lining).

The pleats should be approx. 4.5–5.5cm/1¾–2¼in wide and placed 5cm/2in apart.

1 **Finished size of valance base:** Exactly the same size as the bed base. Cut from lining material, and border it with a piped lip (see below).

2 **Finished drop of bed valance:** From top edge of bed base to carpet.

3 **Fullness of skirt:** 2.5 times around three sides of the bed (excluding the head end).

4 **Cutting length for skirt:** Double 2 above (top edge of bed base to carpet) plus 3cm/1¼in (for two 1.5cm/⅝in seam allowances).

5 **Finished size of lip:** 12cm/5in wide, to run the length of both long sides and along the foot end. Cut from main material.

7 **Finished size of flap at head end:** 20cm/8in × width of bed.

8 **Piping:** Cut strip same as *outside* lengths of finished lip. See no 106.

Bed Headboards

59
BUTTONED HEADBOARDS

A wonderful headboard technique that is easy to execute and very economical. For very little effort and money you can achieve an effective headboard for any bedroom.

All you need is a staple gun, foam rubber, timber, material, lining, buttons, strong thread and braid. The result is a padded headboard covered in the material of your choice, to match the rest of your bedroom furnishings. The button detailing gives both a feeling of depth and a professional look.

The headboard can be attached to most divan-type bed bases: a pair of wooden legs slot over rubber-covered screws at the head end.

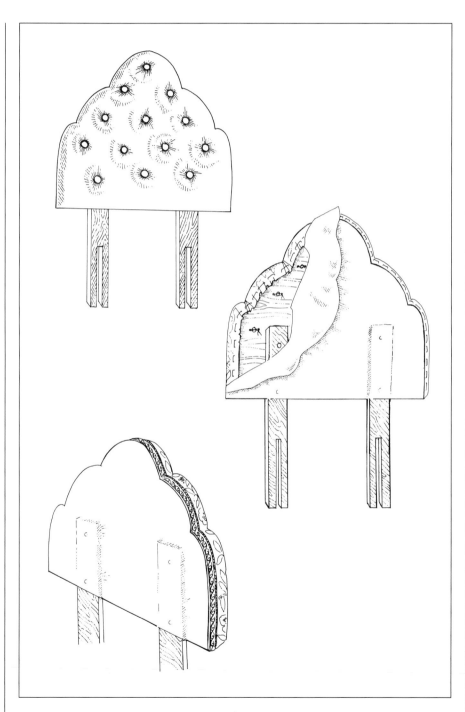

1 **Width of finished headboard:** Width of bed base, plus 3cm/1¼in to accommodate extra width such as a bedcover when it goes over pillows.

2 **Height of finished headboard:** Its highest point should sit approx. 85cm/33½in above the upper surface of the mattress.

3 **Size of timber:** Width and height of 1 and 2 above, cut into a decorative shape (see no 60).

4 **Size of 5cm/2in-thick foam rubber:** As 3 above.

5 **Size of main material:** As 3 above, plus 12cm/5in all the way round each of the four sides.

6 **Size of lining:** As 3 above, plus 2cm/¾in all the way round.

7 **Length of braid:** Enough to go around all four sides of the edge – to cover the staples holding the lining in place. (It is glued in place when the headboard is finished.)

8 **Number of buttons:** Approx 22 (for a double bed).

9 **Size of timber legs:** Two legs, each 1cm/⅜in thick × 4cm/1½in wide × 80cm/31½in long.

60
OTHER HEADBOARD DESIGNS

Coronas, Half-testers and Four-poster Beds

61
BED CORONA

Before you fall in love with the idea of a corona or half-tester above your bed, check that your bedroom is of sufficient size and height to 'take' one. The room needs to be fairly large, and a corona can make a small room look smaller, and cramped. However, if your bedroom has ample room, and a ceiling above 2.3m/7ft 6in tall, this design will be the most beautiful addition, balancing proportions and lifting the eye up from the large, low, rectangular bed.

A corona is supported by a curved board, held up above the bed by metal brackets screwed to the wall. The two side curtains and single back curtain are hung from screw eyes fixed into the underside of the board, and the corona pelmet, hiding the screw eyes, is attached to the board by Velcro. Choose any pelmet style from nos 11 to 37, and use the relevant plan and instructions as your guide. The design pictured is detailed below.

Remember that the corona curtain 'lining' should be of a substantial, attractive material as it is always visible. Therefore the whole curtain is made in a slightly different way to a normal interlined curtain.

The measurements below are suitable for a standard double bed 1.35m (4ft 6in).

BOARD

1 **Dimensions of corona board:** 60cm/ 23½in wide × 48cm/19in deep × 2cm/¾in thick.

2 **Height of board above floor:** Depends on the ceiling height, but 2.3–2.7m/7ft 6in–8ft 10in looks good.

3 **Number of 4cm/1½in brass screw eyes around board:** Approx. 26, screwed in about 5cm/2in apart.

FRONT CURTAINS (2)

4 **Width of each finished, gathered curtain:** Distance between the central screw eye at the front of the board's curve and the corner where the board meets the wall.

5 **Width of each finished, flat curtain:** As 4 above (central screw eye to corner) × 2.5.

6 **Unsewn width of each curtain:** As 5 above (central screw eye to corner × 2.5) plus 5cm/2in for turn-backs at sides (2.5cm/1in at each side).

7 **Length of narrow (3cm/1¼in) gathering tape:** As 5 above (central screw eye to corner × 2.5) plus 4cm/1½in for turnings at sides (2cm/¾in at each side).

8 **Finished drop of each curtain:** Underside of corona board to floor, but narrow gathering tape is placed 4cm/1½in below finished top of curtain.

9 **Unsewn drop for each curtain:** As 8 above – underside of board to floor – plus 4cm/1½in (2cm/¾in for turn-over at top and 2cm/¾in for hem at bottom).

10 **'Lining' quantity:** As width 5. Drop is from underside of board to floor, plus 4cm/1½in: 2cm/¾in turnings both top and bottom.

11 **Interlining quantity:** As width 5 and finished drop 8 above.

BACK CURTAIN (1)

12 **Width of finished, gathered curtain:** 60cm/23½in: width of flat side of corona board.

13 **Width of finished, flat curtain:** Approx. 1.8m/71in.

14 **Unsewn width of each curtain:** As 13 above (approx. 1.8m) plus 5cm/2in for turn-backs at sides (2.5cm/1in at each side). The sides are machined, not hand sewn.

15 **Length of narrow (3cm/1¼in) gathering tape:** As 13 above (approx. 1.8m/71in) plus 4cm/1½in for turnings at sides (2cm/¾in at each side).

16 **Finished drop of curtain:** Underside of corona board to floor.

17 **Unsewn drop of curtain:** As 16 above (screw eyes to floor) plus 4cm/1½in (2cm/ ¾in for turn-over at top and 2cm/¾in for hem at bottom).

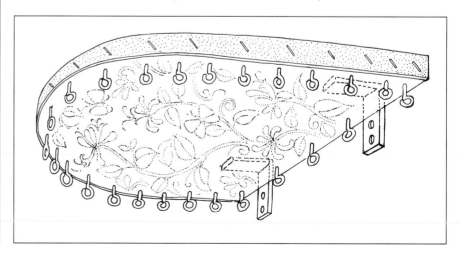

CORONAS, HALF-TESTERS AND FOUR-POSTER BEDS

18 Lining quantity: As width 14 and drop 17 above.

19 Interlining quantity: No need to use interlining.

20 Loop detail: Add a small material loop to either side of back curtain (machined into the seam) at the height where the brass rose will hold back the curtain either side.

PELMET

Gathered skirt off a piped buckram band (see no 26)

21 Finished width of corona pelmet: Length of curved side of corona board (approx 1.28m/50in).

22 Finished drop of corona pelmet: $\frac{1}{6}$ total overall drop from corona board to the floor.

62
HALF-TESTER

A half-tester is also supported by a board supported above the bed by metal brackets screwed to the wall. The two side curtains and single back curtain are hung from screw eyes fixed into the underside of the board, and the pelmet, hiding the screw eyes, is attached to the board by Velcro fastener. Again, it is possible to choose any type of pelmet for the half-tester (see nos 11 to 37). The design pictured is described below.

As with a corona the 'lining' used for the curtains and pelmet must be attractive, and always bring it right up to the edges.

The measurements below are suitable for a standard double bed (1.35m/4ft 6in).

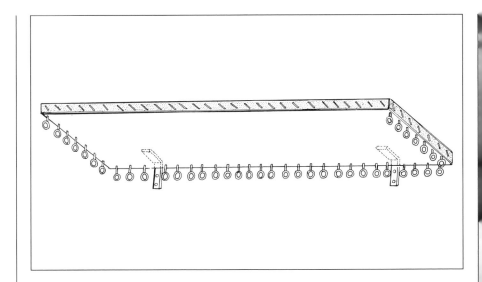

BOARD

1 **Dimensions of half-tester board:** Width of bed × ¼ length of bed × 2cm/¾in thick.

2 **Height of board above floor:** Depends on ceiling height, but between 2.3 and 2.7m/7ft 6in–8ft 10in looks good.

3 **Number of 4cm/1½in brass screw eyes around board:** Approx 40, screwed in about 5cm/2in apart.

SIDE CURTAINS (2)

4 **Width of each finished, gathered curtain:** ¼ length of bed.

5 **Width of each finished, flat curtain:** As 4 above (¼ length of bed) × 2.5.

6 **Unsewn width of each curtain:** As 5 above (¼ length of bed × 2.5) plus 5cm/2in for turn-backs at sides (2.5cm/1in at each side).

7 **Length of narrow (3cm/1¼in) gathering tape:** As 5 above (¼ length of bed × 2.5) plus 4cm/1½in for turnings at sides (2cm/¾in at each side).

8 **Finished drop of each curtain:** Underside of half-tester board to floor.

9 **Unsewn drop for each curtain:** As 8 above (underside of board to floor) plus 4cm/1½in (2cm/¾in for turn-over at top and 2cm/¾in for hem at bottom).

10 **'Lining' quantity:** As width 5 and drop 9 above.

11 **Interlining quantity:** As width 5 and finished drop 8 above.

BACK CURTAIN (1)

12 **Width of finished, gathered curtain:** Width of bed.

13 **Width of finished, flat curtain:** Width of bed × 2.5.

14 **Unsewn width of each curtain:** As 13 above (width of bed × 2.5) plus 5cm/2in for turn-backs at sides (2.5cm/1in at each side).

15 **Length of narrow (3cm/1¼in) gathering tape:** As 13 above (width of bed × 2.5) plus 4cm/1½in for turnings at sides (2cm/¾in at each side).

16 **Finished drop of curtain:** Underside of board to floor.

17 **Unsewn drop of curtain:** As 16 above (underside of board to floor) plus 4cm/1½in (2cm/¾in for turn-over at top and 2cm/¾in for hem at bottom).

18 **Lining quantity:** As width 14 and drop 17 above.

19 **Interlining quantity:** No need to use interlining.

PELMET

Gathered onto Velcro, with fringe (see no 33)

20 **Finished width of pelmet:** Length of 3 sides of half-tester board.

21 **Finished drop of half-tester pelmet:** ⅙ total overall drop from corona board to the floor.

63
FOUR-POSTER BED

With side curtains, gathered pelmet and contrast-bound set-on frill

This is the most beautiful way to dress a four-poster bed: very pretty and full of eye-catching details. The contrast-bound set-on frill perfectly balances the bound, stand-up heading. The back and side curtains are bound at the top in the same contrast, which perfectly relates them to the whole design. All these items for dressing the four-poster are designed and made in such a way that they can be looked at from either side without any turnings, seams or machine lines showing. You must interline everything except the back curtain, which is unnecessary.

It is possible to use a variety of curtains, and pelmet styles (see nos 11 to 37). The instructions below refer to the style pictured.

SIDE CURTAINS (2)

1 Width of each finished, gathered curtain: 50cm/20in. (This is a standard width for almost all four-posters.)

2 Width of each finished, flat curtain: 50cm/20in × 3: 1.5m/60in

3 Unsewn width of each curtain: As 2 above (1.5m/60in) plus 5cm/2in for turn-backs at sides (2.5cm/1in at each side).

4 Length of narrow (3cm/1¼in) gathering tape: 1.5m/60in, plus 4cm/1½in for turnings at sides (2cm/¾in at each side).

5 Finished drop of each curtain: Bottom of four-poster ceiling to carpet.

6 Unsewn drop for each curtain: As 5 above (bottom of four-poster ceiling to carpet) plus 2cm/¾in turn-up at lower edge. The top edge will be contrast bound and top-stitched (which will not show).

7 Lining quantity: As width 3 (1.5m/60in) and drop 6 above.

8 Interlining quantity: As width 3 and finished drop 5 above.

9 Finished width of contrast-bound frill: 6cm/2¼in. See no 105.

10 Length of frill before gathering: As 5 above (bottom of four-poster ceiling to carpet) × 2.5.

11 Size of contrast: 4cm/1½in wide and length as 2 above. Gives 1cm/⅜in showing at the top.

BACK CURTAIN (1)

12 Width of finished, gathered curtain: Width of bed.

13 Width of finished, flat curtain: Width of bed × 2.5.

14 Unsewn width of each curtain: As 13 above (width of bed × 2.5) plus 5cm/2in for turn-backs at sides (2.5cm/1in at each side).

15 Length of narrow (3cm/1¼in) gathering tape: As 13 above (width of bed × 2.5) plus 4cm/1½in for turnings at sides (2cm/¾in at each side).

16 Finished drop of curtain: Bottom of four-poster ceiling to carpet.

17 Unsewn drop of curtain: As 16 above (bottom of ceiling to carpet) plus 2cm/¾in for turn-up at lower edge).

18 Lining quantity: As width 14 and drop 17 above.

19 Interlining quantity: No need to use interlining.

20 Size of contrast: 4cm/1½in wide and length as 13 above. Gives 1cm/⅜in showing at the top.

PELMET

With a gathered/pleated heading, contrast binding at top, decorative rope, and contrast-bound set-on frill

21 Width of flat four-poster pelmet: 3 × 3 sides of the bed (excluding the head end).

22 Unsewn width of pelmet: As 21 above (3 × 3 sides of the bed) plus 5cm/2in for turn-backs at sides (2.5cm/1in at each side).

23 Length of Velcro: 3 sides of the bed.

24 Finished drop of pelmet: ⅙ total overall drop from four-poster ceiling to the floor, plus 5cm/2in stand-up above ceiling of bed.

25 Unsewn drop of curtain: As 24 above (⅙ overall drop plus 5cm/2in) plus 1.5cm/⅝in seam allowance at hem.

26 Lining quantity: As width 22 and drop 25 above.

27 Interlining quantity: As width 22 and finished drop 24 above.

28 Size of contrast binding: 4cm/1½in wide and length as 22 above. Gives 1cm/⅜in showing at the top.

29 Width of finished contrast-bound, set-on frill: 6cm. See no 105.

30 Length of finished contrast-bound, set-on frill: As 21 above (width of flat four-poster pelmet: 3 × 3 sides of the bed) × 2.5.

31 Length of decorative rope: Three sides of the bed, excluding the head end plus 4cm/1½in for finishing off.

CEILING

32 Length of material: Length of the four-poster ceiling, plus 10cm/4in.

33 Width of material: Width of four-poster ceiling × 3. Have it professionally pleated with 2.5cm (1in) lengthways pleats.

Table Covers

64
ROUND TABLE COVER

With deep bullion fringe

A wonderful way of achieving an instant but substantial piece of furniture for relatively little cost. The table made of MDF (medium-density fibreboard) slots and screws together with remarkable ease, and the table cover is very straightforward to make. By choosing a good quality fabric and fringe you can make an extremely elegant piece of furniture for a drawing room, hall or study.

It is mostly possible to machine sew this sort of cover unless, perhaps, the material is very bulky and thick, in which case it is advisable to make it by hand. If you do not want to have to interline the cover, put an old blanket between the table and the lining on the underside.

1 Finished diameter of cover: Height of the table × 2, plus diameter of its top.

2 Unsewn diameter of cover: As 1 above, plus 1.5cm/⅝in all the way round.

3 Lining quantity: As 2 above.

4 Interlining quantity: As 1 above.

5 Length of bullion fringe: Circumference of cover (use formula C=πd, ie ²²/₇ × the total diameter of cover).

6 Drop of bullion fringe: Approx 9cm/3½in looks very elegant.

65
ROUND TABLE COVER

With deep set-on frill

This is made in exactly the same way as no 64, the only difference being the pretty, deep frill, machine stitched on before the cover is lined. Draw a line all the way round the cover for the stitching line, 20cm/8in from the edge. The frill will have a pretty 1.5cm/⅝in stand-up.

This sort of table cover gives a more feminine look than no 64.

1 **Finished diameter of cover:** Height of the table × 2, plus diameter of its top.

2 **Unsewn diameter of cover:** As 1 above, plus 1.5cm/⅝in all the way round.

3 **Lining quantity:** As 2 above.

4 **Interlining quantity:** As 1 above.

5 **Length of finished, gathered frill:** Circumference of cover, 20cm/8in up from lower edge (use formula C=πd, ie ²²⁄₇ × [total diameter of cover, minus 40cm/16in]).

6 **Unsewn length of frill:** As 5 above × 2.5.

7 **Drop of finished frill:** 21.5cm/8½in.

8 **Unsewn drop of frill:** 25cm/10in (to include 2.5cm/1in turn-down at top and 1cm/⅜in for hem at lower edge.

Variation: To contrast bind this frill top and bottom, cut frill 21.5cm/8½in only then cut 2 strips of contrast, 4cm/1½in wide × 6 above (unsewn length of frill).

66
KIDNEY-SHAPED DRESSING TABLE

With inset, overhanging frill

This MDF piece of furniture contains cupboards and drawers and serves a useful purpose in the bedroom. It is very easy to cover, and has a soft, pretty, feminine look.

The single curtain divides in the middle of the front, and draws back on a rail mounted on the underside of the flat top. Do not interline the cover as it will look too heavy.

1 **Width of finished curtain:** Distance around the rail following the kidney shape.

2 **Width of finished, flat curtain:** As 1 above (distance around the kidney-shaped top) × 2.5.

3 **Unsewn width of curtain:** As 2 above (distance around the kidney shape × 2.5) plus 10cm/4in for turn-backs at sides (5cm/2in at each side).

4 **Length of narrow gathering tape:** As 2 above (distance around the kidney shape × 2.5) plus 4cm/1½in for turn-backs at ends (2cm/¾in at each end).

5 **Finished drop for curtain:** Distance from underside of kidney-shaped top to floor.

6 **Unsewn drop for curtain:** As 5 above (distance from underside of top to floor) plus 9cm/3½in (6cm/2¼in for hem – 5cm/2in plus 1cm/⅜in seam with lining – and 3cm/1¼in for turn-down at top).

7 **Lining quantity:** As width 2 above; and drop 5 less 4cm/1½in (due to main material in hem).

8 **Length of finished, gathered frill:** Distance around kidney-shaped top.

9 **Unsewn length of frill:** As 8 above (distance around top) × 2.5 plus 2cm/¾in for seam joining the two ends.

10 **Width of finished frill:** Approx 13cm/5in. Made from doubled-over main material.

11 **Unsewn width of frill:** 29cm/11½in: 26cm/10¼in plus 3cm/1¼in (for 1.5cm/⅝in seam allowance at each edge).

12 **Kidney-shaped top:** Use MDF shape as a template, and add 1.5cm/⅝in seam allowance all the way around.

67
RECTANGULAR DRESSING TABLE

With Velcro-headed curtains

An extremely pretty and simple way of covering any rectangular table. The curtains are attached to the table with Velcro, so it is easy to keep anything unsightly hidden underneath the cover.

1 **Width of finished curtain:** Distance around rectangular top.

2 **Width of finished, flat curtain:** As 1 above (distance around rectangular top) × 3.

3 **Unsewn width of curtain:** As 2 above (distance around top × 3) plus 10 cm/4in for turn-backs at sides (5cm/2in at each side).

4 **Length of Velcro:** As 1 above (distance around rectangular top) plus 10cm/4in extra (for curving round corners, etc).

5 **Finished drop for curtain:** Distance from top of table to floor plus 1cm/⅜in stand-up above the top.

6 **Unsewn drop for curtain:** As 5 above (distance from top of table to floor plus 1cm/⅜in stand-up above the top) plus 10cm/4in (6cm/2¼in for hem – 5cm/2in plus 1cm/⅜in seam with lining – and 4cm/1½in for turn-down at top).

7 **Lining quantity:** As width 2 above; and drop 5 less 6cmm/2¼in (due to main material in hem and stand-up).

8 **Length of decorative rope:** As 1 above (distance around rectangular top) plus 10cm/4in extra (for curving round four corners, etc).

68
TV TABLE COVER

With straight, overhanging valance

*A wonderful way to cover two
extremely ugly pieces of high-tech
equipment – TV and video – in
either a reception room or a bedroom.
The MDF table is well designed and
easy to put together. It is covered by a
single curtain which divides in the
middle of the front, and draws back
on a rail mounted on the underside
of the flat top. The rail is hidden by
the overhanging valance. The success
of the cover depends on your choice of
material and trimming.*

1 **Width of finished curtain:** Distance
around the rail following the circular
shape.

2 **Width of finished, flat curtain:** As 1
above (distance around the circular top) ×
2.5.

3 **Unsewn width of curtain:** As 2 above
(distance around top × 2.5) plus 10cm/4in
for turn-backs at sides (5cm/2in at each
side).

4 **Length of narrow gathering tape:** As
2 above (distance around the top × 2.5)
plus 4cm/1½in for turn-backs at ends
(2cm/¾in at each end).

5 **Finished drop for curtain:** Distance
from underside of top to floor.

6 **Unsewn drop for curtain:** As 5 above
(distance from underside of top to floor)
plus 9cm/3½in (6cm/2¼in for hem –
5cm/2in plus 1cm/⅜in seam with lining –
and 3cm/1¼in for turn-down at top).

7 **Lining quantity:** As width 2 above; and
drop 5 less 6cm/2¼in (due to main
material in hem and stand-up). It is a good
idea to line the cover in an attractive
contrasting material as the lining is visible
when the curtains are opened.

8 **Interlining quantity (optional):**
Width as 3 above, drop as 5 above.

9 **Length of finished overhang:** Distance
around top.

10 **Unsewn length of overhang:**
Distance around top plus 3cm/1¼in for
seam allowances.

11 **Drop of finished overhang:** Approx
10cm/4in. Made from doubled-over main
material.

11 **Unsewn size of overhang:** 23cm/
9¼in: 20cm/8in plus 3cm/1¼in (for
1.5cm/⅝in seam allowance at each edge).

12 **Round top:** Use table top as a
template, and add 1.5cm/⅝in seam
allowance all the way around.

13 **Length of 9cm/3½in bullion fringe:**
As 10 above.

If this TV table cover is too feminine for
your taste, an excellent alternative is to
make an ordinary round table cover – see
no 64. Make the lining from a beautiful
material. To expose the television, pick up
the table cover and fold it over the top to
reveal the lining. It is essential to interline
such a cover, to prevent creasing when the
cover is folded over.

Seat Cushions

69
WINDOW SEAT CUSHION

With foam filling

A window seat is the perfect finish to a feature such as a bay window, a boxed-in radiator (with a brass trellis front) or window recesses in very thick walls.

Foam-filled seat cushions are inexpensive, easy to cover and light to handle – an advantage when turning them over, or removing from direct sunlight in order to arrest fading.

1 **Size of foam rubber:** Exact size of window-seat area and 10cm/4in thick.

2 **Size of material for top and bottom:** Twice the exact size of the foam rubber, plus 2cm/¾in all the way round. (This allows for a 1.5cm/⅝in seam allowance, and 5mm/³⁄₁₆in extra space for the filling.)

3 **Size of material for sides:**

Front and sides: Exact distance around all 3 sides, plus 7cm/2¾in (to allow for turning corners, and seam join. Cut 13cm/ 5in wide (allowing for two seams top and bottom of 1.5cm/⅝in).

Back: Cut exact length of back, plus 3cm/ 1¼in, for 1.5cm/⅝in seams at each corner. Cut 16cm/6¼in wide (allowing for two seams top and bottom of 1.5cm/⅝in; and 1.5cm/⅝in on either side of zip). Cut this piece in half lengthways, to allow for insertion of zip.

4 **Piping quantity:** Two lengths to go right round cushion. See no 106.

5 **Length of zip:** As length of back side of cover.

70
WINDOW SEAT CUSHION

With feather filling and buttons

This type of window seat is even more inviting and decorative than no 69: to sink into a sumptuous feather-filled seat is very comfortable. If the cushion is buttoned as well, it takes on a more organised look.

There is no zip in this seat cover as the buttons prevent its removal from the cushion. Therefore, for cleaning, the whole seat would be dry cleaned.

1 **Size of feather-filled pad:** 12cm/4¾in thick, × exact size of window-seat area plus 10cm/4in in both length and width. This extra size helps the cushion to hold its shape successfully, and to bounce back after being sat upon.

2 **Size of material for top and bottom:** Twice the *exact* size of the window-seat area, plus 1.5cm/⅝in seam allowance all the way round.

3 **Size of material for sides:** Exact distance around all four sides, plus 7cm/ 2¾in (to allow for turning corners, and seam join). Cut 15cm/6in wide (allowing for two seams of 1.5cm/⅝in).

4 **Piping quantity:** Two lengths as 3 above. See no 106.

5 **Buttons:** Use 25mm/1in-wide self-covering metal buttons. Quantity depends on the size of the window seat, but they should be spaced about 25–30cm/10–12in apart.

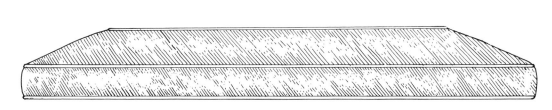

Foam-filled seat cushion

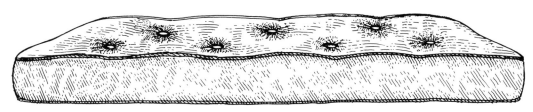

Feather-filled, buttoned seat cushion

Tie-backs and Hold-backs

71
BUCKRAM
SCALLOPED TIE-BACK

With piping

These look good in any situation, and although they look somewhat dated now, deserve a definite place in design history.

They are more difficult to make than the softer, more contemporary tie-backs. They are mostly hand sewn, stiffened by thick, brown pelmet buckram with interlining on both sides of it. Although main fabric is used on both sides, it is still a fairly economical tie-back as such a small quantity of fabric is needed.

1 **Length of tie-back:** This depends on the width of curtain to be held back. Once your curtains are hanging, take a tape measure and get someone else to hold it loosely around the curtain in the manner of a tie-back. Always position the tie-back lower rather than higher; level with the window sill, or possibly a window seat, is a good guide, but **not** a rule, as the window sill may be rather high. The fact that someone else is holding the tape measure means that you can walk to the end of the room and judge the size, length and position of the tie-back from afar.

2 **Width of tie-back:** 12cm/5in average.

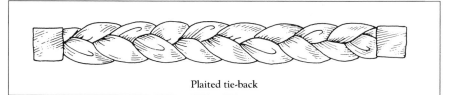

Plaited tie-back

72
PLAITED TIE-BACK

These look particularly good when the window treatment includes some type of gathered pelmet, but especially one that might involve a plaited or ruched band in its design. They look brilliant in any room and should not be thought of as essentially feminine in character.

The tie-back is made of three tubes of material, stuffed with interlining. It is largely machine made and is so quick and easy. It looks very effective when one of the three strips is done in a contrast to the main material.

1 **Length of tie-back:** See no 71. When the tie-back is plaited, 25% of the length will be lost, so be sure to add at least this much to the desired finished length.

2 **Width of tubes:** Cut material approx. 9cm/3½in wide, so that after sewing with a 1.5cm/⅝in seam, the finished tubes are 3cm/1¼in wide. The tubes can be cut narrower or wider than this, depending on how thick or thin you desire the plait.

3 **Size of interlining:** Cut strips of interlining that are 50% wider than the material tubes, and the same length. Drop them into the tube using a piece of string and a weight. There is no need to roll or fold them in any way.

Buckram scalloped tie-back

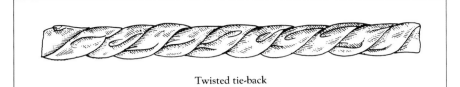

Twisted tie-back

73
TWISTED TIE-BACK

These are made in a similar way to the Plaited Tie-back (see no 72), except that two tubes are used instead of three. This tie-back is considerably more masculine than the plaited one. It looks most effective when one tube is in the main material and the other is in a contrast.

1 **Length of tie-back:** See no 71. When the tie-back is twisted 25% of the length will be lost, so be sure to add at least this much to the desired finished length.

2 **Width of tubes:** Cut material approx. 9cm/3½in wide, so that after sewing with a 1.5cm/⅝in seam, the finished tubes are 3cm/1¼in wide. The tubes can be cut narrower or wider, depending on how thick or thin you wish the twist to be.

3 **Size of interlining:** Cut strips of interlining that are 50% wider than the material tubes, and the same length. Drop them into the tube using a piece of string and a weight.

4 **Backing for twist:** Once finished, you need to anchor the tie-back by hand, sewing it to a narrow buckram band. Cut a strip of fusible buckram approx. 2.5cm/1in wide, and the same length as the twist. Cover it in a tube of the main material, before stitching the twist to it.

74
CATERPILLAR TIE-BACK

Simple to make, but very effective. As with the plaited tie-back (no 72), this tie-back can echo ruching in a pelmet or pole-headed curtain. It uses quite a lot of fabric: three times the length of the finished band for most materials, but six times if using silk.

1 **Length of tie-back:** See no 71. Cut 3 × desired finished length.

2 **Width of tubes:** Cut material approx. 12cm/5in wide, so that after sewing with a 1.5cm/⅝in seam, the finished tube is approx. 5cm/2in wide.

3 **Size of interlining:** 18cm/7in wide (50% wider than material strip). Cut exactly the finished length of tie-back.

75
CATERPILLAR TIE-BACK

With ears

The description of no 74 also applies to this tie-back. This design, however, has added impact due to its extra dimension.

1 **Length of tie-back:** See no 71. Cut 3 × desired finished length.

2 **Width of tubes:** Cut material approx. 16cm/6¼in wide, so that after sewing with a 1.5cm/⅝in seam, the finished tube is 6.5cm/2½in wide. This then allows 1cm/⅜in either side for the ears.

3 **Size of interlining:** 18cm/7in. Cut exactly the finished length of tie-back.

76
CATERPILLAR TIE-BACK

With contrast ears

The description of no 74 also applies to this tie-back. The extra detail of a contrast colour for the ears gives more interest and a greater depth to the tie-back.

1 **Length of tie-back:** See no 71. Cut 3 × desired finished length.

2 **Unsewn width of main material strips (2):** 7cm/2¾in.

3 **Unsewn width of contrast-colour strips (2):** 4cm/1¾in. Join with 1cm/⅜in seams to give 1cm/⅜in-wide contrast once folded in half.

4 **Size of interlining:** 18cm/7in. Cut exactly the finished length of tie-back.

Caterpillar tie-back

Caterpillar tie-back with ears

Caterpillar tie-back with contrast ears

77
BOW TIE-BACK

These are very charming and pretty, and obviously have a very feminine appearance. They should never be found in a reception room but are purely for bedrooms and bathrooms.

They are made from two wide sashes (use long ones for maximum elegance) which have rings at each end that are unhooked each time the tie-back is used, so that the bow does not have to be constantly re-tied. Never interline the sashes as it would ruin the bow's crisp, light appearance.

1 Length of tie-back: See no 71. A good length for each sash is 1.1m/3ft 6in.

2 Unsewn width of sash: 22cm/8½in, to be folded in half lengthways. Use a 1cm/⅜in seam.

3 Finished width of sash: 10cm/4in.

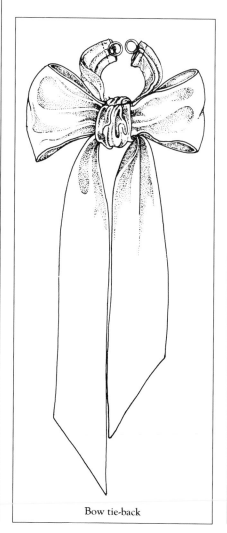

Bow tie-back

78
KNOT TIE-BACK

The description of no 77 also applies to this tie-back, although it is somewhat less pretty and feminine than the bow. However, its soft appearance and sashes still make it largely unsuitable for reception rooms.

1 Length of tie-back: See no 71. A good length for each sash is 1.1m/3ft 6in.

2 Unsewn width of sash: 22cm/8½in, to be folded in half lengthways. Use a 1cm/⅜in seam.

3 Finished width of sash: 10cm/4in.

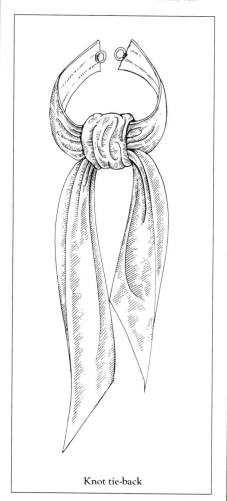

Knot tie-back

79
BRASS ROSE HOLD-BACK

Sometimes, the style of a window treatment is enhanced by a piece of brass window furniture as opposed to a fabric tie-back. Brass roses are particularly fitting, for example, for holding back the front curtains of a corona.

Brass roses consist of a flat, ornamental disc, and a thinner metal shank which screws into the wall. Department stores sell them in varying styles and sizes.

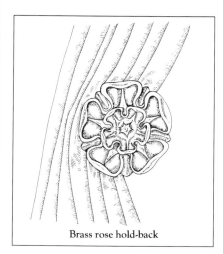

Brass rose hold-back

80
BRASS ARM HOLD-BACK

Another style of window furniture. They are particularly useful when there are right-angled walls or cupboards too close to the window frame to accommodate a material tie-back. In these situations a neat, tight brass arm is perfect for holding back curtains. They also work well when used with curtains on brass swing arms (see no 9).

They are manufactured in various styles and lengths.

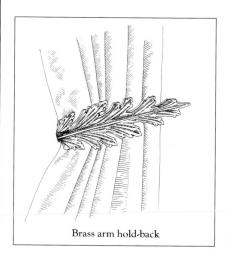

Brass arm hold-back

Rosettes and Bows

81
MALTESE CROSS

The most elegant of all the rosettes, and perfect for both reception rooms and bedrooms. Never interline them as it would spoil the crisp, light look which is so effective. They are largely machine made.

1 Size of vertical strip: 26 × 47cm/9 × 18½in

2 Size of horizontal strip: 26cm × 45cm/ 9 × 17¾in

3 Button: 15–20mm/⁶⁄₁₀–¾in looks best.

Maltese cross

82
MALTESE CROSS

With contrast binding

The contrast binding adds an extra dimension to this style of Maltese cross, and ties in well with the same contrast in a pelmet or curtain.

1 Size of vertical strip, main material: 13 × 47cm/5 × 18½in

2 Size of vertical strip, contrast material: 16 × 47cm/6¼ × 18½in

3 Size of horizontal strip, main material: 13 × 45cm/5 × 17¾in

4 Size of horizontal strip, contrast material: 16 × 45cm/6¼ × 17¾in

5 Button: 15–20mm/⁶⁄₁₀–¾in looks best.

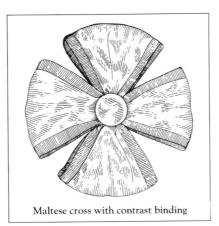

Maltese cross with contrast binding

83
CHOUX ROSETTE – EXPLOSIVE

A particularly pretty type of rosette suitable for both reception rooms and bedrooms, with a very 'light' look to it. It is entirely hand sewn and easy to make.

1 Diameter of finished rosette: 10cm/ 4in.

2 Size of main material: 30cm/12in square.

3 Size of main material for backing: 12cm/5in diameter circle. (Fold in 1cm/ ⅜in all the way round.)

4 Size of buckram and interlining: 10cm/4in diameter circles. Cut one in fusible or pelmet buckram; two in interlining. Fusible buckram is easier on the fingers.

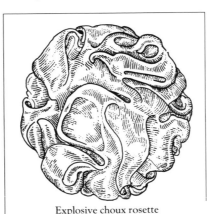

Explosive choux rosette

84
CHOUX ROSETTE – CONTROLLED

This type of rosette has a slightly stronger presence than the explosive type. It is therefore a highly suitable detail to add to a window treatment involving a fixed-head curtain, Austrian blind or a pelmet – especially when dealing with a large window.

1 Diameter of finished rosette: 10cm/ 4in.

2 Size of main material: 35cm/14in square.

3 Size of interlining: 35cm/14in square.

4 Size of main material for backing: 12cm diameter circle. (Fold in 1cm/⅜in all the way round.)

5 Size of buckram, and interlining at back: 10cm/4in diameter circles.

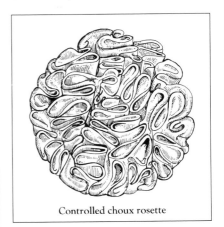

Controlled choux rosette

85
BOW

A pretty and feminine detail suitable for a bedroom, bathroom or young girl's room. It adds the perfect finishing touch to the centre of a pelmet or the corner of an Austrian blind. Never interline a bow.

1 Finished width of bow: Approx. 12cm/5in.

2 Finished length of sashes: 12cm/5in.

3 Unsewn size of strip: 15cm/6in × 1m/ 3ft 3in. (To be folded in half.)

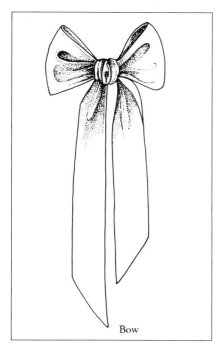

Bow

86
FLOWER ROSETTE

With contrast binding

An effective rosette that is quick and simple to make, being mostly machine made. Contrast binding on both sides of the strip of material looks particularly effective, especially when the same contrast is already present in, for example, frilling.

1 Diameter of finished rosette: 10cm/ 4in.

2 Size of main material: Strip 8 × 45cm/ 3¼ × 18in .

3 Size of contrast strips (2): 4 × 45cm/ 1½ × 18in.

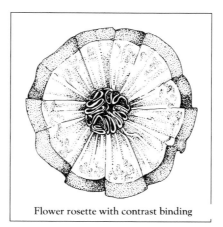

Flower rosette with contrast binding

87
BUTTONED ROSETTE

Another form of rosette, suitable for a pelmet or an Austrian blind. The use of the rosette can often have the effect of pulling the whole window treatment together.

  Never interline a rosette as it would spoil its light, crisp look.

1 Diameter of finished rosette: Approx. 14cm/5½in.

2 Size of main material: Strip 14 × 49cm/ 5½ × 19¼in.

3 Button: 25mm/1in.

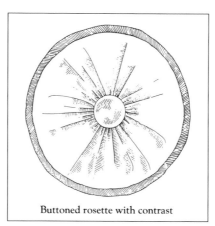

Buttoned rosette with contrast

88
BUTTONED ROSETTE

With contrast

Similar to no 87, but has more depth to it due to the contrast layer.

1 Diameter of finished rosette: Approx. 15cm/6in.

2 Size of main material: Strip 14 × 45cm/ 5½ × 18in.

3 Size of contrast material: Strip 15 × 49cm/6 × 19¼ in.

4 Button: 25mm/1in.

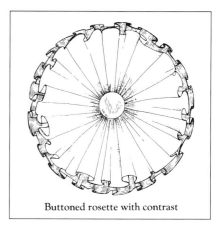

Buttoned rosette with contrast

Blinds

89
AUSTRIAN BLIND

With pencil pleats and gathered frill

This is an excellent window treatment when some sort of curtain is needed, but you want to keep space free under a window. It is perfect in a kitchen or bathroom to clear units below window sills, or in children's bedrooms so that valuable space under the window can then be used for a toybox, book shelf, desk or doll's cot, etc. Also, if you are unlucky enough to have had a builder or architect who insisted on putting radiators under windows, this type of blind may be a solution. Austrian blinds also work well in dormer windows when the adjacent walls do not allow housing space for curtains. However the dormer should be quite tall (and south or west facing) otherwise the blind would take up too much light.

Austrian blinds are always hung using Velcro from a wooden batten approx. 5 × 2.5cm/2 × 1in, which is fixed to the wall above the window. The batten should be the exact width of the window plus an extra 5cm/2in on either side.

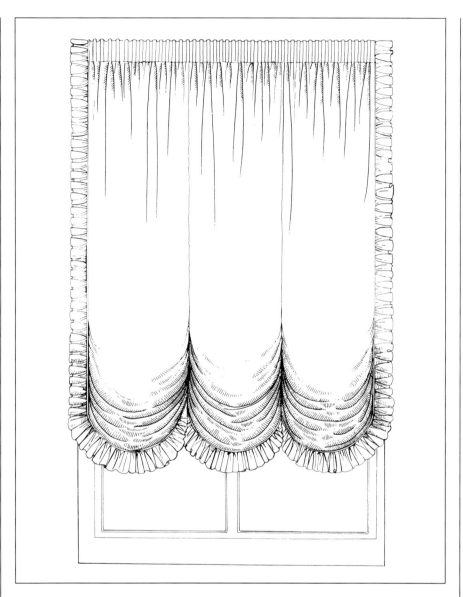

1 **Width of finished, gathered blind:** Exact length of batten, plus the width of the frill, approx 5cm/2in on either side, and to extend slightly beyond the batten.

2 **Width of finished, flat blind:** 2–2.5 × the width of the batten.

3 **Unsewn width of blind:** As 2 above (2.5 × width of batten) plus 3cm/1¼in for seam allowances: 1.5cm/⅝in at each side.

4 **Length of pencil-pleat gathering tape:** The exact width of the finished, flat blind, plus 4cm for turning in of tape (2cm/¾in on either end).

5 **Finished drop of blind (including frill):** From top of batten to 30cm/12in below sill. This extra is for the permanent swag effect when the blind is fully down.

6 **Unsewn drop of blind:** As 5 above (top of batten to 30cm/12in below window sill) plus 9.5cm/3¾in: 8cm/3¼in turn-down at top and 1.5cm/⅝in seam allowance at bottom.

7 **Lining quantity:** Height from batten to bottom of blind, plus 1.5cm/⅝in seam allowance.

8 **Hanging length of blind (when fully down, but swagging):** From top of batten to just below sill, or just on to unit or radiator below window.

9 **Length of gathered frilling:** Exact measurement of 2 drops and 1 width of the flat blind.

10 **Unsewn length of frill:** 2.5 × 9 above.

11 **Cord quantity:** Swags in blinds tend to be approx. 40cm/15¾in wide. For each row of rings the cord must go from the bottom, turn a right angle through a screw eye at the top and go across to the right-hand top corner of the batten, then half-way down the right-hand side.

12 **Number of 4cm/1½in screw eyes:** Same as number of swags, plus 1.

13 **Spacing of 1.5cm/⅝in plastic rings:** 20cm/8in.

90
AUSTRIAN BLIND

With inverted pleats

*See no 89 – the same details apply
here. This is a simple and understated heading for an Austrian
blind. The inverted pleats lie flat,
and the three edges are plain. The
design works beautifully in any
fabric – even linen.*

1 **Width of finished, pleated blind:**
Exact length of batten used to hang blind.

2 **Width of finished, flat blind:** 2.5 × the
width of the batten.

3 **Unsewn width of blind:** As 2 above
(2.5 × width of batten) plus 3cm/1¼in for
seam allowances: 1.5cm/⅝in at each side.

4 **Finished drop of blind:** From top of
batten to 30cm/12in below window sill.
This additional allowance is for the swag
effect when the blind is fully down.

5 **Unsewn drop of blind:** As 4 above
plus 3cm/1¼in: 1.5cm/⅝in seam
allowance at top and bottom.

6 **Lining quantity:** As unsewn width 3
and unsewn drop 5 above.

7 **Hanging length of blind (when fully
down, but swagging):** From top of batten
to just below sill, or just on to unit or
radiator below window.

8 **Cord quantity:** Swags in blinds tend to
be approx. 40cm/15¾in wide. For each
row of rings the cord must go from the
bottom of the blind, turn a right angle
through a screw eye at the top and go
across to the right-hand top corner of the
batten, then half-way down the right-hand
side.

9 **Number of 4cm/1½in screw eyes:**
Same as number of swags, plus 1.

10 **Spacing of 1.5cm/⅝in plastic rings:**
20cm/8in.

91
AUSTRIAN BLIND

On a pelmet board with tails and two swags

This type of blind is suited to all the situations described under no 89, but is constructed in a different way. The blind is made fuller than normal and hung on a pelmet board projecting out 12cm/5in. To make the tails, the strings that pull up the blind are placed 20cm/8in in from the edges of the blind. Frilling or trimming is essential to accentuate the interesting shape.

1 **Width of finished, gathered blind (including frills):** Exact length of pelmet board, plus its returns.

2 **Width of finished, flat blind:** 2.5 × the width of board, including its returns.

3 **Unsewn width of blind:** As 2 above (2.5 × width of board) plus 3cm: 1.5cm/⅝in for seam allowance at each side.

4 **Length of pencil-pleat gathering tape:** The exact width of the finished, flat blind, plus 4cm/1½in for turning in of tape: 2cm/¾in on either end.

5 **Finished drop of blind (including frill):** From top of pelmet board to 30cm/12in below window sill. This additional allowance is for the swag effect when the blind is fully down.

6 **Unsewn drop of blind:** As 5 above (top of batten to 30cm/12in below window sill) plus 9.5cm/3¾in: 8cm/3¼in turn-down at top and 1.5cm/⅝in seam allowance at bottom.

7 **Lining quantity:** As unsewn width 3 and unsewn drop 6 above.

8 **Hanging length of blind (when fully down, but swagging):** From top of board to just below sill, or just on to unit or radiator below window.

9 **Length of gathered frilling:** Exact measurement of 2 drops and 1 width of the flat blind.

10 **Unsewn length of frill:** 2.5 × 9 above.

11 **Cord quantity: 3 rows of rings:** For each row of rings the cord must go from the bottom of the blind, turn a right angle through a screw eye at the top and go across to the right-hand top corner of the batten, then half-way down the right-hand side.

12 **Number of 4cm/1½in screw eyes:** 4.

13 **Spacing of 1.5cm/⅝in plastic rings:** 20cm/8in.

92
AUSTRIAN BLIND

On a pelmet board with tails and one swag

A similar style to no 91, which looks particularly elegant when used 'dressed': that is, not pulled up or down each day, but left half-down all the time with its swags and curves beautifully arranged. It should be trimmed in a fine, long fringe of linen or cotton to enhance its shape.

1 **Width of finished, gathered blind (including frills):** Exact length of pelmet board, plus its returns.

2 **Width of finished, flat blind:** 2.5 × the width of board, including its returns.

3 **Unsewn width of blind:** As 2 above (2.5 × width of board) plus 3cm: 1.5cm/⅝in for seam allowance at each side.

4 **Length of pencil-pleat gathering tape:** The exact width of the finished, flat blind, plus 4cm/1½in for turning in of tape: 2cm/¾in on either end.

5 **Finished drop of blind (including frill):** From top of pelmet board to 30cm/12in below window sill. This additional allowance is for the swag effect when the blind is fully down.

6 **Unsewn drop of blind:** As 5 above (top of batten to 30cm/12in below window sill) plus 9.5cm/3¾in: 8cm/3¼in turn-down at top and 1.5cm/⅝in seam allowance at bottom.

7 **Lining quantity:** As unsewn width 3 and unsewn drop 6 above.

8 **Hanging length of blind (when fully down, but swagging):** From top of board to just below sill, or just on to unit or radiator below window.

9 **Length of fringe:** Exact measurement of 2 drops and 1 width of the flat blind.

10 **Cord quantity:** 2 rows of rings: For each row of rings the cord must go from the bottom of the blind, turn a right angle through a screw eye at the top and go across to the right-hand top corner of the batten, then half-way down the side.

11 **Number of 4cm/1½in screw eyes:** 3.

12 **Spacing of 1.5cm/⅝in plastic rings:** 20cm/8in.

93
LONDON BLIND

This is an excellent window treat-
ment in special circumstances: when
a window is fairly small, or very slim.
This type of blind is often used to
screen an ugly city view, such as a
brick wall or an unsightly courtyard
– hence its name. It is also useful as
the second element in a window
treatment, framed by curtains and a
pelmet.

A London Blind can be made as a
sheer, or in thicker material and
lined. Like an Austrian or a Roman
blind, it is hung from a batten, and is
pulled up with cords threaded
through plastic rings sewn on at the
back. It is very economical on mate-
rial, and is quick and easy to make,
requiring no fusible buckram or
commercial tape, just Velcro.

The blind is more decorative than
functional, as it looks best left
hanging long rather than pulled up.
A small amount of cord can be
pulled up (and secured to a cleat or
hook) to create the pleasing shape at
the lower edge.

1 Width of finished blind: The exact
width of the window recess or frame.

2 Unsewn width of blind: As 1 above
(exact width of window) plus 10cm/4in:
(5cm/2in for turn-backs at each side), plus
20cm/8in per inverted pleat. Place the
inverted pleats about 22cm/8½in apart.
These blinds usually have only two pleats,
or sometimes three.

3 Finished drop of blind: From top of
batten to window sill (if in a window
recess), or lower (if not in a recess).

4 Unsewn drop of blind: As 3 above,
plus 10cm/4in (5cm/2in for turnings at
both top and bottom).

5 Unsewn lining width: As 2 above
(width of window, plus 10cm/4in for turn-
backs, plus 20cm/8in per pleat).

6 Unsewn lining length: As 3 above
(finished drop of blind).

7 Cord quantity: For each inverted pleat
and row of rings you will need a cord to
pull the blind up. It must go from the
bottom of the blind, turn a right angle
through a screw eye at the top and go
across to the right-hand top corner of the
batten, then half-way down the side.

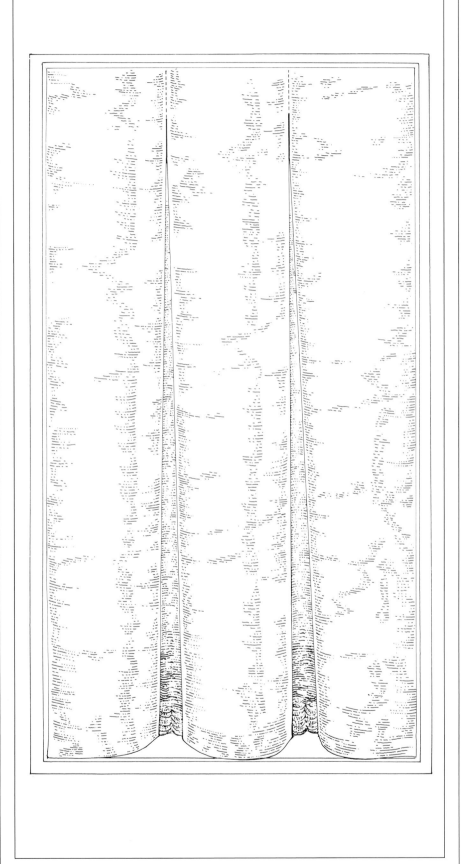

8 Number of 4cm/1½in screw eyes:
Same as number of cords, plus 1.

9 Spacing of 1.5cm/⅝in plastic rings:
15cm/6in.

94
ROMAN BLIND

This blind will always deserve a special place in design history due to its plain, understated look. It can be used on its own as a complete window covering, or as one of the elements in a more complicated design, such as in a bay window with a pelmet and dress curtains.

Roman blinds are very economical on fabric as there is no gathering or pleating. They can look very plain, or be made highly decorative by adding special details (see nos 97 and 98). They are hung using Velcro from a batten in the same way as Austrian blinds, and their even folds are supported by thin wooden rods spaced about every 20cm/8in down the blind.

1 **Width of finished blind:** The exact width of the window recess or frame.

2 **Unsewn width of blind:** As 1 above (exact width of window) plus 10cm/4in (5cm/2in for turn-backs at each side).

3 **Finished drop of blind:** From top of batten to window sill (if in a window recess), or lower (if not in a recess).

4 **Unsewn drop of blind:** As 3 above, plus 10cm/4in (5cm/2in for turnings at both top and bottom).

5 **Unsewn lining width:** As 1 above (exact width of window). (3cm/1¼in will be turned in on each side.)

6 **Unsewn lining length:** As 3 above (finished drop of blind) plus 5cm/2in per rod channel, plus 2cm/¾in for turning under Velcro at top of blind.

7 **Size of dowelling rods:** Length as 1 above (exact width as window) minus 6cm/2¼in, × 1.5cm/⅝in diameter.

8 **Size of timber batten (inserted in hem):** 1 × 4cm/⅜ × 1½in × width of blind minus 2cm/¾in.

9 **Cord quantity:** Unless your blind is more than 1.35m/4ft 6in wide, you will only need two cords to pull it up, each placed approx 12cm/5in from the edge. For each row of rings the cord must go from the bottom of the blind, turn a right angle through a screw eye at the top and go across to the right-hand top corner of the batten, then half-way down the right-hand side.

10 **Number of 4cm/1½in screw eyes:** Same as number of cords, plus 1.

95
ROMAN BLIND

With contrast border

See no 94 – the same details apply. However, the added detail here makes the blind more interesting to look at, and makes a slightly stronger statement. This involves precise measurement and sewing and the finished blind would be ruined by any errors. However, the result is well worth the effort involved.

1 **Width of finished blind:** The exact width of the window recess or frame.

2 **Unsewn width of blind:** As 1 above (exact width of window). (The edges are to be bound, and so do not need hem or seam allowances.)

3 **Finished drop of blind:** From top of batten to window sill (if in a window recess), or lower (if not in a recess).

4 **Unsewn drop of blind:** As 3 above.

5 **Unsewn lining width:** As 1 above (exact width of window). (3cm/1¼in will be turned in on each side.)

6 **Unsewn lining length:** As 3 above (finished drop of blind) plus 5cm/2in per rod channel, plus 2cm/¾in for turning under Velcro at top of blind.

7 **Size of dowelling rods:** Length as 1 above (exact width of window) minus 6cm/2¼in, × 1.5cm/⅝in diameter.

8 **Size of timber batten (inserted in hem):** 1 × 4cm/⅜ × 1½in × width of blind minus 2cm/¾in.

9 **Cord quantity:** Unless your blind is more than 1.35m/4ft 6in wide, you will only need two cords to pull it up, each placed approx 12cm/5in from the edge. For each row of rings the cord must go from the bottom of the blind, turn a right angle through a screw eye at the top and go across to the right-hand top corner of the batten, then half-way down the right-hand side.

10 **Number of 4cm/1½in screw eyes:** Same as number of cords, plus 1.

11 **Contrast strips:** Cut the length of all four sides × 13cm/5in. Machine on, with raw edges together 4cm/1½in from the edge to form a 4cm/1½in binding, mitred at the corners. You will have 5cm/2in to turn over at back of blind.

96
TIMBER PELMET BOARDS FOR USE WITH BLINDS

Roman blinds are such a minimal window treatment that they may benefit from added detail such as a timber pelmet board. They are easy to make using timber and an electric jigsaw.

Many variations in design are possible, using shape, colour and texture. Extra decorative details can be added, such as gold balls at downward points, tiny brass motifs like fleurs-de-lys or painted lines following the design. Such a board effectively crowns a Roman blind and makes a strong conclusive statement.

Size of timber board: Approx 24cm/9½in depth at front × width of blind × 10cm/4in return into the wall.

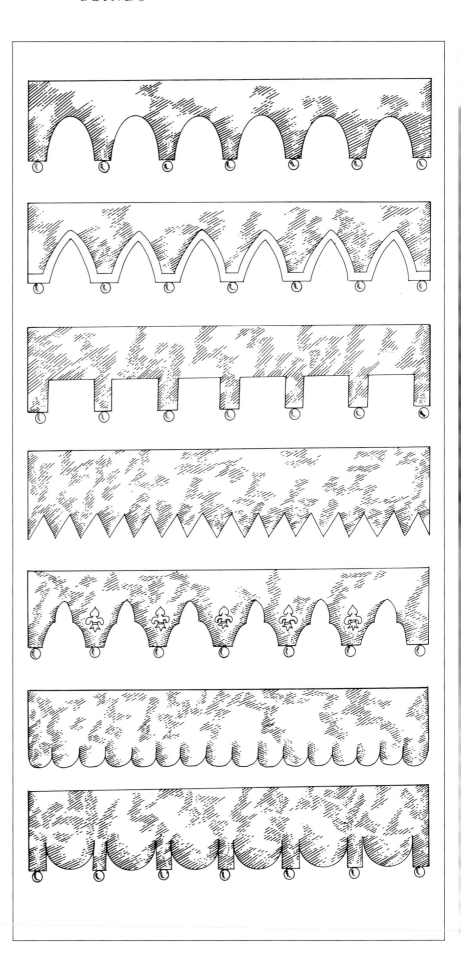

97
ROMAN BLIND

With contrast braid, under a wooden board

See no 94 – the same details and instructions apply here.

To add the braid, draw a line 4cm/1½in from the edge down the two sides and along the bottom, then top stitch the braid on before making up the blind.

1 Width of finished blind: The exact width of the window recess or frame.

2 Unsewn width of blind: As 1 above (exact width of window) plus 10cm/4in (5cm/2in for turn-backs at each side).

3 Finished drop of blind: From top of batten to window sill (if in a window recess), or lower (if not in a recess).

4 Unsewn drop of blind: As 3 above, plus 10cm/4in (5cm/2in for turnings at both top and bottom).

5 Unsewn lining width: As 1 above (exact width of window). (3cm/1¼in will be turned in on each side.)

6 Unsewn lining length: As 3 above (finished drop of blind) plus 5cm/2in per rod channel, plus 2cm/¾in for turning under Velcro at top of blind.

7 Size of dowelling rods: Length as 1 above (exact width as window) minus 6cm/2¼in, × 1.5cm/⅝in diameter.

8 Size of timber batten (inserted in hem): 1 × 4cm/⅜ × 1½in × width of blind minus 2cm/¾in.

9 Cord quantity: Unless your blind is more than 1.35m/4ft 6in wide, you will only need two cords to pull it up, each placed approx 12cm/5in from the edge. For each row of rings the cord must go from the bottom of the blind, turn a right angle through a screw eye at the top and go across to the right-hand top corner of the batten, then half-way down the right-hand side.

10 Number of 4cm/1½in screw eyes: Same as number of cords, plus 1.

11 Braid quantity: 3 sides around blind.

98
ROMAN BLIND

With contrast border and fans, under a scalloped wooden board

This blind has enormous depth and interest due to its highly decorative details. The shape of the wooden board should exactly echo the fans on the lower edge of the blind. The design allows the introduction of curves into an otherwise totally rectangular, hard-edged window treatment.

1 **Width of finished blind:** The exact width of the window recess or frame.

2 **Unsewn width of blind:** As 1 above (exact width of window). (The edges are to be bound, and so do not need hem or seam allowances.)

3 **Finished drop of blind:** From top of batten to window sill (if in a window recess), or lower (if not in a recess).

4 **Unsewn drop of blind:** As 3 above.

5 **Unsewn lining width:** As 1 above (exact width of window). (3cm/1¼in will be turned in on each side.)

6 **Unsewn lining length:** As 3 above (finished drop of blind) plus 5cm/2in per rod channel, plus 2cm/¾in for turning under Velcro at top of blind.

7 **Size of dowelling rods:** Length as 1 above (exact width of window) minus 6cm/2¼in, × 1.5cm/⅝in diameter.

8 **Size of timber batten (inserted in hem):** 1 × 4cm/⅜ × 1½in × width of blind minus 2cm/¾in.

9 **Cord quantity:** Unless your blind is more than 1.35m/4ft 6in wide, you will only need two cords to pull it up, each placed approx 12cm/5in from the edge. For each row of rings the cord must go from the bottom of the blind, turn a right angle through a screw eye at the top and go across to the right-hand top corner of the batten, then half-way down the right-hand side.

10 **Number of 4cm/1½in screw eyes:** Same as number of cords, plus 1.

11 **Contrast strips:** Cut the length of all four sides × 13cm/5in. Machine on, with raw edges together 4cm/1½in from the edge to form a 4cm/1½in binding, mitred at the corners. You will have 5cm/2in to turn over at back of blind.

12 **Fan width:** Divide blind to give fans of approx 12–25cm/5–10in width. Fans that measure ⅕ of total width look excellent.

13 **Unsewn size for fan:** Cut width according to 11 above, plus 3cm/1¼in: 1.5cm/⅝in seam allowance on each side). Length should equal fan width × 22%. Each fan needs double material. Pleat up on ironing board with a hot iron and hand stitch to hold in place.

99
LAMBREQUIN

With roller blind

Sometimes windows that are small, slim or low are not suitable for any form of curtain treatment. A lambrequin – a hardboard, covered 'frame' – with a roller blind behind is the perfect, elegant solution.

1 **Finished width of lambrequin:** Exact window width plus 10cm/4in.

2 **Finished length of lambrequin:** Exact window width plus 8cm/3¼in.

3 **Width of covering material:** Exact window width plus 20cm/8in.

4 **Length of covering material:** Exact window width plus 16cm/6¼in.

5 **Interlining quantity:** Enough to cover exact face of lambrequin only.

6 **Size of hardboard:** As 1 and 2 above. Use a paper template to cut out shape.

7 **Battens for back of lambrequin:** Each 5 × 2.5cm/2 × 1in. One as width 1 above; two as length 2 above. Screw the hardboard shape onto the battens, then cover the entire structure in the chosen material using a non-staining heavy-duty glue (eg Hitac). In some places, it is possible to use a staple gun, but the staples must not be visible when the lambrequin is attached to the wall.

8 **Flush brackets:** 4 (2 for each vertical batten).

9 **Roller blind** (professionally made). Use same main material. Ensure the lower edge echoes the shape of the lambrequin top. To fit exact recess of the window.

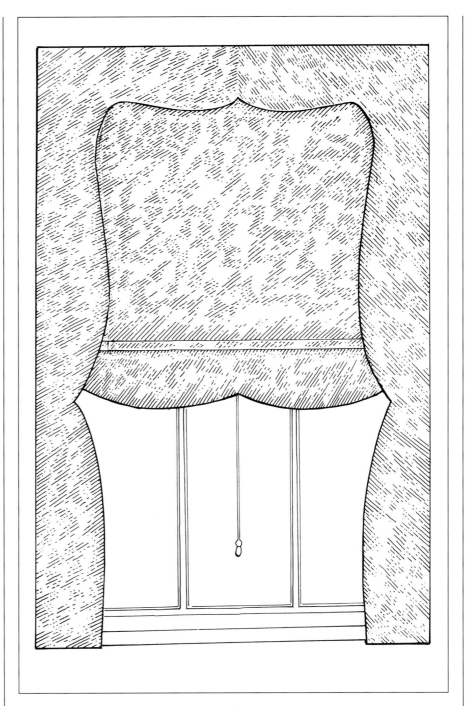

100
LAMBREQUIN

With braid detail and roller blind

See no 99 – the same details and instructions apply here.
   To add the braid, draw a line 3cm/1¼in in from the edge of the finished lambrequin shape.

10 **Braid quantity:** Measure line drawn on lambrequin, plus 10cm/4in for corners and turnings. Glue onto line once lambrequin is finished.

Sheers

101
VOILE SHEER

Off a brass rod

This sheer curtain can serve as an entire window treatment on its own, or it can be a lovely second layer behind a set of curtains or an Austrian blind. It is the perfect solution when privacy is required, or it can be used as a beautiful decorative element.

The curtain is not divided in the centre, and is not designed to be opened in any way. The brass rod is held up with cord, screw eyes and a brass cleat. Not only is this the correct and elegant way of hanging these sheers but it also facilitates removal for cleaning.

1 **Width of each finished, gathered sheer:** The exact size of the window recess.

2 **Width of each finished, flat sheer:** As 1 above (exact size of window) × 1.5.

3 **Unsewn width of each sheer:** As 2 above (exact size of window × 1.5) plus any necessary seam allowances. The curtain edges should be left as selvedges. Seams should be avoided but if absolutely necessary, sew French seams.

4 **Length of brass drop rod:** As 1 above: exact size of window recess less 2cm/¾in.

5 **Finished drop for each sheer:** Height from brass rod to bottom of window recess.

6 **Unsewn drop for each sheer:** Height as 5 above (from brass rod to bottom of window recess) plus 19.5cm/7½in: 13.5cm/5¼in for stand-up head and channel for rod at top (all doubled over) and 6cm/2¼in for doubled-over 3cm/1⅜in hem at bottom.

7 **Brass screw eyes (4cm/1½in):** 2, for channelling cord in two top corners of recess.

Variation: Another way of hanging a sheer (made of voile, lace or silk) is to use a second working curtain rail hung behind the front rail and set right back in the window recess. This can create privacy if needed, but can be drawn back, if desired. Use no 2 as a guide for your curtain, but do not use either lining or interlining. Therefore all side seams and the hem can be machine stitched.

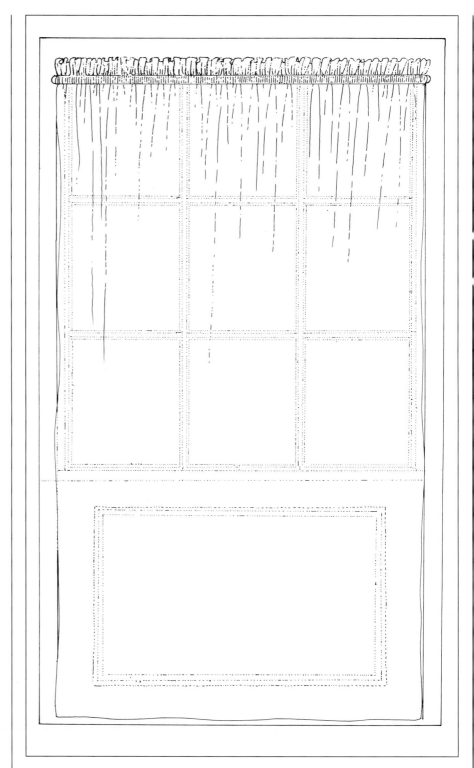

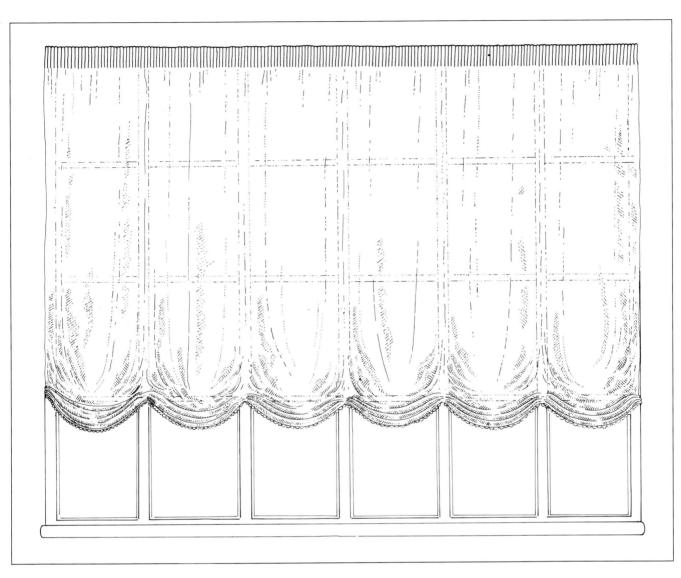

102
SHEER AUSTRIAN BLIND

Another way of providing privacy, or of just adding a decorative element to a window treatment.

The blind is made in the same way as no 89, but is unlined, to preserve the sheer look. The inverted pleats make a suitable heading instead of anything more complicated.

The sides should ideally be left as selvedges. Hems should be as small as possible, and rolled rather than folded before hand stitching.

1 **Width of finished, pleated blind:** Exact length of batten used to hang blind.

2 **Width of finished, flat blind:** 2.5 × the width of the batten.

3 **Unsewn width of blind:** As 2 above (2.5 × width of batten) plus and seam allowance necessary. Avoid having any seams, and leave the edges as selvedges. If seams are absolutely necessary, have them running down the same lines as the plastic rings, and sew them as French seams.

4 **Finished drop of blind:** From top of batten to 30cm/12in below window sill. This additional allowance is for the swag effect when the blind is fully down.

5 **Unsewn drop of blind:** As 4 above plus 3cm/1¼in: 1.5cm/⅝in seam allowance at top and bottom.

6 **Hanging length of blind (when fully down, but swagging):** From top of batten to just below sill, or just onto unit or radiator below window.

7 **Cord quantity:** Swags in blinds tend to be approx. 40cm/15¾in wide. For each row of rings the cord must go from the bottom of the blind, turn a right angle through a screw eye at the top and go across to the right-hand top corner of the batten, then half-way down the right-hand side.

8 **Number of 4cm/1½in screw eyes:** Same as number of swags, plus 1.

9 **Spacing of 1.5cm/⅝in plastic rings:** 20cm/8in.

Frills and Piping

103
INSET FRILL

This frill is made from material folded in half lengthways, wrong sides and raw edges together. It can be gathered or pleated by hand on the machine, and is then inserted in a 1.5cm/⅝in seam. It may or may not be piped (see below).

1 Width of finished frill (standard): 6cm/2¼in.

2 Unsewn width of frill: 15cm/6in.

3 Ungathered length of frill: Length of item to be trimmed × 2.5. (Join strips with 1.5cm/⅝in seams.)

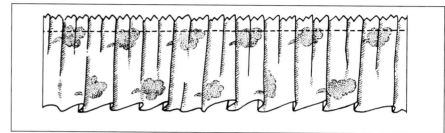

104
PERMANENT-PLEATED INSET FRILL

A very elegant frill, and a favourite for trimming pelmets. Make the required length of flat material then send off to a commercial pleater for 4mm/⅛in pleating (or for a bolder effect, 8mm/¼in).

1 Width of finished frill (standard): 6cm/2¼in.

2 Unsewn width of frill: 9cm/3¼in. (Includes 1.5cm/½in seam at top and 1.5cm/½in turn-up on lower edge.)

3 Ungathered length of frill: Length of item to be trimmed × 3 plus 4mm/1½in for turnings either end. (Join strips with 1.5cm/⅝in seams.)

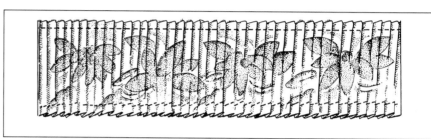

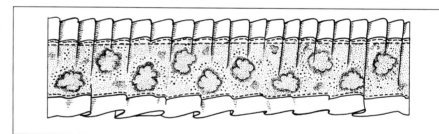

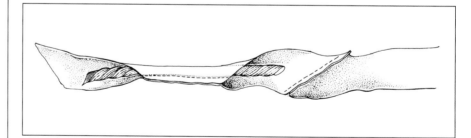

105
CONTRAST-BOUND SET-ON FRILL

This is made from a double layer of material where the main material and contrast are sewn into a tube, right sides and raw edges together

with a 5mm/¼in seam. The contrast is 1cm/⅜in wider than the main colour so that when the frill is turned right side out and pressed flat (before gathering) 5mm of contrast shows at the top and bottom.

1 Width of finished frill (standard): 6cm/2¼in.

2 Width of main material: 7cm/2¾in.

3 Width of contrast: 8cm/3¼in.

4 Ungathered length of frill: Length of item to be trimmed × 2.5. (Join strips with 1.5cm/⅝in seams.)

106
PIPING

1 Unsewn width of material: 4cm/1½in. Cut on the bias or cross of material.

2 Length of material: Length of item to be piped plus 4cm/1½in (2cm/¾in for turnings at either end). (Join shorter strips with 1.5cm/⅝in seams.)

3 Length of piping cord (pre-shrunk): Length of item to be piped plus 4cm/1½in extra.

Suppliers

TABLE CLAMPS AND FOLDING RULERS

UK
Lady Caroline Wrey
60 The Chase
London SW4 ONH
Tel: 071 622 6625

USA
Greentext Upholstery Supplies
236 West 26 Street
New York
NY 10001
Tel: 212 206 8585

CHINTZES AND OTHER MATERIALS

UK
Hallis and Hudson Group Ltd
Bushell Street
Preston
Lancs PR1 2SP
Tel: 0772 202202
Fax: 0772 889889

Just Fabrics
Burford Antique Centre
Cheltenham Road
Burford
Oxon OX18 4JA
Tel: 0993 823391
Fax: 0993 822751

USA
ArtMark Fabric
480 Lancaster Pike
Frazer
PA 19355

Gige Interiors, Ltd
(see Curtain-hanging Materials)

Norbar Fabrics
PO Box 810938
Boca Raton
FL 33481-0938
Tel: 1 800 645 8501

INTERLININGS AND LININGS

UK
Hesse and Co
7 Warple Mews
Warple Way
London W3 ORF
Tel: 081 746 1366
Fax: 081 746 2366

Hunter and Hyland Ltd
(see Curtain-hanging Materials)

Porter Nicholson
Portland House
Norlington Road
London E10 6JX
Tel: 081 539 6106
Fax: 081 558 9200

USA
Gige Interiors, Ltd
(see Curtain-hanging Materials)

CURTAIN-HANGING MATERIALS

UK
Hunter and Hyland Ltd
201–5 Kingston Road
Leatherhead
Surrey KT22 7PB
Tel: 0372 328511
Fax: 0372 370038

USA
Gige Interiors Ltd
170 S. Main Street
Yardley
PA 19067
Tel: 215 493 8052

Springs Window Fashions
(Graber Products)
7549 Graber Road
Middleton
WI 53562
Tel: 1 800 356 9102

Kirsch Co
PO Box 370
Sturges
MI 49091
Tel: 1 800 528 1407

HKH Design
24 Middlefield Drive
San Francisco
CA 94132
Tel: 415 564 2385

SEWING EQUIPMENT

UK
John Lewis Partnership
(all branches)
278–306 Oxford Street\
London W1A 1EX
Tel: 071 629 7711
Fax: 071 629 0849

USA
Calico Corners (national chain)
Funwood Everfast Inc
Walnut Road Business Park
203 Gale Lane
Kennett Square
PA 19348
Tel: 215 444 8700

TABLE BASES, DRESSING AND TV TABLES

UK
The Dormy House
Sterling Park
East Portway
Andover
Hants SP10 3TZ
Tel: 0264 365808
Fax: 0264 366359

USA
Minic Custom Woodwork, Inc
524 East 117th Street
New York
NY 10035
Tel: 212 410 5500
Fax: 212 410 5533

Hoot Judkins
1142 Sutter Street
San Francisco
CA 94109
Tel: 415 673 5454

PERMANENT PLEATERS

UK
Ciment Pleating
39B Church Hill Road
Off Church Hill
Walthamstow
London E17 9RX
Tel: 081 520 0415
Fax: 081 520 9047

USA
SF Pleating
425 Second Street
San Francisco
CA 94107
Tel: 415 982 3003

ROLLER BLINDS

UK
Decorshades
5 Brewery Mews Business Centre
St John's Road
Isleworth
Mddx, TW7 6PH
Tel/Fax: 081 847 1939

TRIMMINGS

UK
G J Turner and Co
Fitzroy House
Abbot Street
London E8 3DP
Tel: 071 254 8187
Fax: 071 254 8471

USA
M&J Trimmings
1008 Sixth Avenue
New York
NY 10018
Tel: 212 391 9072

Index